C000071973

s:

k
re the last
n or ask for
it to be renewed.

L32

W O
V

R
M

GERALD

27 JAN 1992
-9 MAR 1992   21 AUG 1993
-6 OCT 1992

10 SEP 1993

17 OCT 1992   8 OCT 1993
10-17-92
JAN 1993   30 JUL 1994

•DOMINO•

First published in 1991

Apart from any fair dealing for the purposes of research or private study, or criticism or review, as permitted under the Copyright, Designs and Patents Act, 1988, this publication may only be reproduced, stored or transmitted, in any form or by any means, with the prior permission in writing of the publishers, or in the case of reprographic reproduction in accordance with the terms of licences issued by the Copyright Licensing Agency. Enquiries concerning reproduction outside those terms should be sent to the publishers at the undermentioned address:

Kogan Page Limited
120 Pentonville Road
London N1 9JN

© The Domino Consultancy Ltd

British Library Cataloguing in Publication Data

A CIP record for this book is available from the British Library.

ISBN 0 7494 0519 8

Typeset by DP Photosetting, Aylesbury, Bucks
Printed and bound in Great Britain by
Clays Ltd, St Ives plc

Contents

Preface

Welcome to our new series of three books under the title The Women in Management Workbook Series.

This first book, *Are You Ready to Manage?* has been written for women seeking their first management appointment, whether it be managing a team of people or managing a function. It helps you to assess your skills, qualities and experience, and looks at ways you can boost your confidence. It also considers the various methods you can use to find that first appointment, as well as how to settle into your new role.

The second in the series, entitled *The Successful Manager* assesses the different ways you can make a success of your management post. It considers assertiveness and communication at work, how to manage your team, and how to manage your time.

The third book, called *Getting to the Top*, considers the steps you can make to gain promotion. It looks at breaking down the barriers to advancement, leadership skills, and how to get the most out of talks, meeting and interviews. It also evaluates various tactics for promotion.

The premise of this series is twofold:

- That women in the 1990s are actively seeking management posts of all kinds.
- That women have the ability to fulfil these posts but sometimes lack the self-confidence and the necessary support to move on and up.

These books, all written by women, contain practical advice on how to get where you want to be. There are ideas and tips which can be adapted for your own unique purposes. The books are full of case studies — women already in management positions explaining how certain techniques helped them.

The books are to be read proactively — in other words, to get the most out of them, you have to get involved. So read with a pen in your hand. There are charts and checklists for you to complete — each one taking you further towards your personal management goal!

We wish you every success in your management career.

Geraldine M Bown
Managing Director
The Domino Consultancy Limited

The Women in Management Workbook Series

The Domino Consultancy Ltd

A series of three self-assessment workbooks devised specifically for women aiming for a career in management. Each workbook deals with a specific stage in a woman's management career using the same 'action learning' approach which allows for a surprising level of self-awareness. Other titles in the series are:

WORKBOOK 2:   THE SUCCESSFUL MANAGER

Aimed at those women who have attained a management position, this book shows how to achieve excellence and professionalism in their work by improving skills in important areas such as communication, team building, time management and assertiveness.

ISBN 0 7494 0518 X

WORKBOOK 3:   GETTING TO THE TOP

The final book in the series is for those women who have proved themselves as successful managers but are now focused on joining the ranks of senior management. Topics covered include leadership skills, tactics for promotion, stress management and presentations.

ISBN 0 7494 0517 1

The Domino Consultancy

The Domino Consultancy Ltd is recognised particularly in the UK and abroad for their expertise in the highly specialised and growing area of women's training and development. They are well known for their high quality training materials and their client base includes NatWest, Midland, Barclays and TSB Banks; Shell UK; the AA; Scottish Homes; PowerGen; Harrods; Manchester Airport; Safeway and Marks and Spencers.

Geraldine Bown is the managing director of Domino, the vice president of the European Women's Management Development Network and representative to the European Women's lobby. She is a frequent speaker at conferences here and abroad.

Catherine Brady is a director of Domino and is responsible for all its development and production projects.

While both being successful business women, the authors each have families and, therefore, firsthand experience of balancing the demands of home and work.

Introduction

What is a Manager?

You are probably reading this book (or flicking through the pages in the bookshop) because you want to move into management. But are you clear about what the term means and what the job is likely to entail?

The simple answer is that there is no clear definition of the term 'manager'. Some people consider themselves to be managers when they are not. Others would never dream of calling themselves managers when, in fact, that is exactly what they are.

A manager is most commonly defined as a person who directs and controls the work of other people; for example, managing an office, department or section. However it is equally valid to define a manager as a person who directs and controls a function; for example, managing finance, administration, or even a computer system.

In many cases the management post does not even carry the 'manager' title. Management jobs range from the very grand title of 'director' to 'officer', 'administrator' and 'controller'. In fact there is a whole host of titles which come under the umbrella of 'manager'. This can make job hunting confusing - particularly when you have little or no experience of the organisation or field of work you are interested in.

There is help at hand. Mintzberg (1973) identified three basic functions of managers — interpersonal, informational and decisional. He then broke the function down into ten separate roles. All management jobs comprise one or more of these ten roles. They are:

Interpersonal

1.   Figurehead — to undertake certain duties as a representative of the company.

2.   Leader — to lead a team of subordinates.

3.   Liaison — to build and maintain relationships with groups outside the company.

Informational

4.   Monitor — to identify progress and problems, trends and opportunities, and to take appropriate action.

5.   Disseminator — to circulate information throughout the company from both internal and external sources.

6.   Spokesperson — to pass information about the organisation to the outside world from within the organisation.

Decisional

7.   Entrepreneur — to plan and control change within an organisation.

8.   Disturbance handler (sometimes called troubleshooter) — to cope with unforeseen crises.

9.   Resource allocator — to provide the tools, whether it be money, time or equipment, to allow planned activities to take place.

10.   Negotiator — to acquire resources from external companies or other departments.

These roles may seem a little daunting, particularly if you are taking the first steps to a career in management. They should not. Whether you are currently in paid work or not, you fulfil many of these roles now ... maybe without even realising it. Here are two examples.

Naomi

Naomi is personal assistant to the managing director of a small engineering works. She has been in the role for three years and feels she is ready to move into a junior management position. However, she is worried about her lack of experience.

Some of her present responsibilities include controlling the petty cash (negotiator), producing weekly sales reports for sales meetings (monitor), and ordering office supplies at discount prices (liaison and negotiator). Once, when her manager was ill, she gave a talk to senior secretaries on the sales database the company uses (figurehead and spokesperson).

Naomi is ready for management!

Annette

Annette formerly worked in the civil service before taking eight years off to bring up her children. Now that the children are at school, she wishes to return to a management post but fears her skills are rusty — or, worse still, non-existent.

In her present role she has brought up two quarrelsome children (leader and disturbance handler) and has been active in the local playgroup, maintaining a register of local child-minders (liaison). She has organised fund-raising events and headed the committee deciding how the funds should be spent (entrepreneur and resource allocator). She has taken total control, not just of bringing up her children, but of managing and controlling every aspect of the household (the list of roles here is endless!).

These two women have just the skills needed in management. The skills they have accumulated both at home and at work can be directly transferred into a management position. The problem is, they do not realise it.

Do you?

The main purpose of this book is to prepare you for a management post. It will help you assess your own skills and look at ways of increasing your confidence. Once you know what you can do and feel confident in your abilities, it considers how to match your skills to the jobs available. This is followed by advice on how to apply for a job and how to handle the all-important interview. There is also advice on how to survive the first few hours/days/weeks of your new job. Finally, you will draw up an action plan. This covers the steps *you* are going to take in your preparations for management.

There's plenty of opportunity for self-assessment, so have a pen or pencil close at hand.

Happy reading and happy hunting!

1

Assessing Yourself

As a first step in preparing to manage, you must assess your potential to manage. In other words, be aware of the skills, qualities and knowledge you can bring to a management post. Realising your own talents this way helps to boost your inner confidence through the recognition that *you are skilled*. It also helps you accurately to match yourself to the type of management positions which are currently available.

This chapter helps you to assess your skills, qualities and knowledge as they derive from the roles you adopt, the personal experiences you have undergone, the jobs you have had, and the skills base you have developed.

ROLES

Women are capable of adopting many roles. Inside work, women have to be planners, organisers, team leaders and motivators, and must, therefore, be very flexible and versatile. Outside work, there are numerous other roles women adopt. Consider yours now.

List all the roles you now have and have had in the past — including work, social, domestic and community. Some ideas are given overleaf, but there may be many others.

Possible roles

girlfriend	wife
daughter	friend
mother	customer
traveller	sports player
committee member	fund raiser
carer	chairperson
party giver	cook
cleaner	neighbour
sick visitor	speaker
singer	actress
interior designer	nurse
decorator	gardener
problem-solver	rule maker
chauffeur	mechanic
listener	comforter
family organiser	judge and jury

My roles:

trainer - NTL. Girlfriend. wife
daughter. Friend. Mother
Customer. cook. cleaner
neighbour. listener
Comforter
family organiser

You may be surprised at how many roles you have — and at the variety. The good thing about roles is that they develop skills and qualities which can be used in other contexts. Even those roles which are imposed by external forces, such as nursing sick children or visiting an elderly relative, all add to a woman's skills base.

Here is an example of one woman's roles as mother, partner, homemaker, cook and friend. Write in all the skills that she has used during the day in her out-of-work roles.

The first box has been completed as an example.

Case study: a day in the life of Anita

Time	Tasks	Skills
7.00 am	Gets up. Gets the children up. Prepares breakfast. Writes a letter for child to give to teacher, explaining absence on previous day.	organising communicating planning letter-writing
8.00 am	Sorts out a squabble between children as to who takes the last apple to school.	
8.30 am	Leaves key with neighbour for plumber who is to repair washing machine. Takes children to school.	
9.00 am	Arrives at work.	
12.30 pm	Lunch break. Makes a dental appointment for one of children. Calls at the bank for a statement of account. Checks the statement over a sandwich in the office.	
3.00 pm	Finishes work. Calls at the butcher's on the way home to get some meat for tea and tells him how much the family enjoyed the meat she bought at the weekend.	
3.30 pm	Collects the children from school. Drops the youngest child at friend's house to play. Buys a birthday card for partner's mother. Arranges with her sister to babysit when Anita and her partner go out tomorrow.	

4.30 pm	Rings plumber to complain that the washing machine is still leaking. Told that a visit is impossible before tomorrow afternoon. After discussion, visit is arranged first thing tomorrow morning. Organises tea.	
6.00 pm	Arranges for partner to do the supermarket shopping as Anita is going to keep-fit session with friend. Writes a shopping list before leaving.	
6.30 pm	Picks friend up.	
8.30 pm	Arrives home.	
9.00 pm	Helps son with maths homework.	
9.30 pm	Tries to persuade daughter to leave TV and go to bed.	
9.45 pm	Friend rings in an emotional state. Calms her down and arranges to meet her tomorrow lunch-time.	
10.00 pm	Daughter goes to bed. Watches TV and listens to partner's problems at work.	
11.00 pm	Makes a list of things to do tomorrow.	

These are the skills that could have been included:

Case study: a day in the life of Anita

Time	Tasks	Skills
7.00 am	Gets up. Gets the children up. Prepares breakfast. Writes a letter for child to give to teacher, explaining absence on previous day.	organising communicating planning letter-writing
8.00 am	Sorts out a squabble between children as to who takes the last apple to school.	negotiating solving conflict
8.30 am	Leaves key with neighbour for plumber who is to repair washing machine. Takes children to school.	planning organising delegating
9.00 am	Arrives at work.	time management
12.30 pm	Lunch break. Makes a dental appointment for one of children. Calls at the bank for a statement of account. Checks the statement over a sandwich in the office.	planning time management financial assessment
3.00 pm	Finishes work. Calls at the butcher's on the way home to get some meat for tea and tells him how much the family enjoyed the meat she bought at the weekend.	feedback motivation giving praise
3.30 pm	Collects the children from school. Drops the youngest child at friend's house to play. Buys a birthday card for partner's mother. Arranges with her sister to babysit when Anita and her partner go out tomorrow.	planning organising decision-making research

4.30 pm	Rings plumber to complain that the washing machine is still leaking. Told that a visit is impossible before tomorrow afternoon. After discussion, visit is arranged first thing tomorrow morning. Organises tea.	negotiating scheduling problem-solving assertiveness
6.00 pm	Arranges for partner to do the supermarket shopping as Anita is going to keep-fit session with friend. Writes a shopping list before leaving.	delegating planning
6.30 pm	Picks friend up.	caring
8.30 pm	Arrives home.	
9.00 pm	Helps son with maths homework.	motivating numerical skills teaching
9.30 pm	Tries to persuade daughter to leave TV and go to bed.	negotiating persuading
9.45 pm	Friend rings in an emotional state. Calms her down and arranges to meet her tomorrow lunch-time.	coping with crisis counselling listening setting priorities
10.00 pm	Daughter goes to bed. Watches TV and listens to partner's problems at work.	listening supporting
11.00 pm	Makes a list of things to do tomorrow.	planning setting goals setting priorities

Women with children are likely to have all these skills! Statements such as 'I've been out of work for five years having a family, so I'm afraid I'm out of touch' are *out*, to be replaced by 'I've been bringing up a family for the last five years, and this has given me many skills which I would now like to transfer back to the workplace.'

And it is not just skills. Skills are important to an employer, but just as important are personal qualities and knowledge. Both of these factors are built up at the same time as your skills base.

Just as your work and home life give you skills, qualities and knowledge, so do your roles in the community, your social life or your hobbies. Consider these now.

Group together your roles under headings such as Family, Community, Social, Sports, etc, and fill in the blank table. An example is given opposite.

Assessing yourself: roles

Roles	Skills, qualities, knowledge
Family *wife*	counsellor, listener, supporter, sharer, financial management, crisis management, delegator, risk taker
partner	compromiser, negotiator, sharer
daughter	carer, nurse, patience, awareness of needs of others
sister	handling jealousy, competitor, supporter

Assessing yourself: roles

Roles	Skills, qualities, knowledge

Now that you have considered how roles have added to your skills/qualities/knowledge base, move on to personal experiences.

PERSONAL EXPERIENCES

Personal experiences are the past events in your life which hold special significance for you, and through which you learned something about yourself. They might include caring for a terminally ill family member, surviving a personal crisis, having a spell in hospital, or acting calmly in an accident. They might be experiences which other people do routinely but which, for you, represent significant events. All experiences play a major part in determining the sort of person you are now, and where you are capable of going in the future. It's easy to underestimate the importance of what has happened to you in the past. Now is the time to take stock.

Fill in the blank table, listing the skills, qualities, and knowledge your personal experiences have given you. As before, an example is provided.

Assessing yourself: personal experiences

Personal experiences	Skills, qualities, knowledge
caring for terminally ill person	tenacity, surviving loss of someone very dear, getting the most out of every day, nursing skills, listening
breakdown of marriage	coping with failure and rejection, understanding my own needs and wants, planning for the future financially, enjoying my own company

Assessing yourself: personal experiences

Personal experiences	Skills, qualities, knowledge

Now that you have built up a list of skills, qualities and knowledge from your roles and experiences, move on and look at the jobs you have had, and what you learned from them.

JOBS

How long this exercise takes you will depend upon how old you are and how many jobs you have had!

Fill in the table in the same way as the others. This time there are two models — one from a 26-year-old secretary, who, before she tried this exercise, said she had done nothing of value since she had left school; and the other from a personnel and recruitment manager, who did the exercise in order to prepare for an important interview.

The following are some examples from their sheets.

Assessing yourself: jobs — Sue

Jobs	Skills, qualities, knowledge
Machinist	<ul><li>planning shirt outlays</li><li>industrial machining</li></ul>
Telesalesperson	<ul><li>selling appliances</li><li>customer service</li><li>book-keeping</li></ul>
Stewardess	<ul><li>waitress</li><li>reception duties</li><li>bar work</li><li>planning evening functions</li></ul>
Administrator	<ul><li>shipping documentation</li><li>invoicing</li><li>telexing and teletyping</li><li>supervising distribution</li></ul>
Secretary	<ul><li>managing a small office</li><li>typing invoices</li><li>telesales</li><li>scheduling deliveries</li><li>stock control</li></ul>

Assessing yourself: jobs — Penny

Jobs	Skills, qualities, knowledge
First job: insurance clerk	<ul><li>customer service</li><li>telephone answering/ communication</li><li>handling verbal and written enquiries</li><li>filing</li><li>record keeping</li><li>applying policy/admin procedures to insurance requests</li><li>working out quotations</li><li>preparing policies</li><li>handling complaints</li><li>teamwork</li></ul>gained:<ul><li>insight into world of work</li><li>realisation of need for accuracy and precision</li><li>an appreciation of the importance of teamwork</li><li>determination to get a degree</li><li>realisation of how important time management is</li></ul>
Latest job: personnel and training manager	Personnel skills used and teamwork developed. Also learned:<ul><li>how to survive in a political environment</li><li>self-reliance</li><li>decision making</li><li>risk analysis and risk taking</li><li>assertiveness</li><li>to take responsibility for decisions</li><li>to sell ideas</li><li>that being a manager means not always being popular</li><li>the importance of pursuasive and influencing ability</li></ul>

Assessing yourself: jobs

Jobs	Skills, qualities, knowledge

You should have a fair array of skills, qualities and knowledge based on your life to date, even without mentioning qualifications or formal examinations. You may have included these formal qualifications yourself on one of the sheets you have completed, but they have been omitted here because their importance is more obvious.

These exercises were intended to assess skills and qualities — ones that you will certainly want a future employer to know about. Before moving on, make sure you have highlighted all the skills you could apply to a management post, particularly your people skills. The next exercise will help you do this.

SKILLS BASE

On the next few pages is a skills check-list. Tick every skill you think you have. There are two columns: 'OK' and 'Good'. No standards have been set, only whether you can do the things that are listed, and which things you are better at than others.

Carry out the exercise quickly — it should not take longer than 10 minutes. If you are unsure about any of these skills, give yourself the benefit of the doubt. You will then have an opportunity to assess the results.

Management skills check-list

	Please tick one	

Assertiveness skills	OK	Good
Expressing appreciation readily		✓
Expressing compliments		✓
Receiving compliments		✓
Saying 'no' without feeling guilty	✓	
Asking for help	✓	
Asking for information		✓
Disagreeing with someone	✓	
Giving criticism	✓	
Responding to criticism	✓	
Speaking up in meetings	✓	
Speaking in front of a group	✓	
Requesting good service	✓	
Expressing justified anger	✓	
Expressing justified displeasure	✓	
Accepting a rejection	✓	
Responding to a 'put-down'	✓	
Making and maintaining eye contact in conversation		✓
Entering a room full of strangers		✓
Stating your views to an authority figure		✓
Refusing to allow yourself to be manipulated		✓
Telling people how you feel		✓
Stating your view clearly		✓
Accepting different opinions		✓

Communication skills	OK	Good
Listening intently		✓
Listening accurately		✓
Editing		✓
Communicating clearly in speech		✓
Communicating clearly in writing		✓
Thinking quickly on one's feet	✓	
Explaining difficult concepts or ideas		✓
Giving clear instructions		✓
Making yourself understood in a foreign language	✓	
Translating		
Teaching a foreign language		
Writing minutes		✓
Dealing well with the public		✓
Summarising		✓
Writing copy for press/marketing/advertising		
Writing with humour, fun or flair	✓	
Writing a good letter		✓
Writing a good speech		
Giving a good talk	✓	
Writing proposals		✓
Writing publicity		
Speaking well on the telephone		✓
Starting a conversation	✓	
Ending a conversation	✓	
Interviewing		✓
Being interviewed		✓

Interpersonal skills	OK	Good
Being helpful to friends		✓
Being helpful to strangers		✓
Solving arguments	✓	
Understanding how others feel		✓
Talking easily with all kinds of people		✓
Nursing		
Showing people you care about them		✓
Offering support		✓
Providing comfortable and pleasant surroundings		✓
Anticipating people's needs		✓
Working well with a team		✓
Encouraging people		✓
Working well with people of different status, values, race, sex, etc		✓
Sharing credit with others		✓
Dealing patiently with difficult people		✓
Working well in a hostile environment		✓
Understanding family relationships and problems		✓
Representing others		
Apologising when necessary		✓
Controlling your temper		✓
Sizing up a situation quickly		✓
Being approachable		✓
Carrying out performance appraisals		✓
Sizing up a person quickly		✓

Leadership skills	OK	Good
Beginning new tasks, ideas, projects		✓
Taking the first move in relationships		✓
Recruiting		
Getting people to work together		
Negotiating		
Inspiring trust		✓
Persuading people	✓	
Promoting change	✓	
Taking risks	✓	
Taking difficult decisions	✓	
Carrying out decisions		✓
Seizing opportunities		✓
Spotting problems		✓
Solving problems		✓
Challenging ideas and actions		✓
Dealing well with crises		✓
Working well under stress		✓
Using imagination	✓	
Figuring out new ways of doing things		✓
Showing good judgement		✓
Applying theory to practice		✓
Doing new things on one's own		✓
Evaluating team effectiveness		
Assessing people's needs		
Building a team		
Using the skills of others	✓	
Supervising others	✓	
Judging people's effectiveness		✓
Giving feedback		✓
Assessing the potential of others		✓

Planning and organising skills	OK	Good
Meeting deadlines		✓
Making and using contacts	✓	
Making it easier for other people to be organised		✓
Organising information in a systematic way		✓
Delegating	✓	
Coordinating tasks		✓
Managing time		✓
Making arrangements		✓
Deciding on priorities		✓
Planning meetings of any kind		✓
Finding ways to speed up a job		✓
Working unsupervised		✓
Setting goals		✓
Setting standards		✓
Setting deadlines		✓
Setting alternatives		✓
Improvising/adapting ideas		✓
Handling a variety of tasks and responsibilities		✓
Setting up control systems so that deadlines can be met		✓
Recognising the talents of others		✓

Learning and information skills	OK	Good
Finding out about things you didn't know		✓
Observing people/data/behaviour		✓
Concentrating		✓
Questioning		✓
Scanning		
Learning quickly		✓
Assimilating a lot of information		✓
Remembering things		✓
Reading quickly		✓
Recognising need for more information		✓
Researching		✓
Investigating		✓
Gathering information		✓
Analysing information		✓
Classifying information		✓
Selecting relevant information		✓
Checking information		✓
Keeping records		✓
Storing information		✓
Filing		✓
Retrieving information		✓
Tracing problems to source		✓
Reviewing large amounts of information and summarising briefly		✓
Seeing the relationship between cause and effect		✓
Organising information in a systematic way		✓
Keeping confidential information		✓

Training skills	OK	Good
Explaining		✓
Teaching		✓
Advising		✓
Coaching		✓
Helping people to develop themselves		✓
Counselling		✓
Leading a group	✓	
Running a training session	✓	

Performance skills	OK	Good
Getting up before a group	✓	
Demonstrating		✓
Speaking at meetings	✓	
Stimulating enthusiasm	✓	
Acting		
Conducting ceremonies		
Striking up conversations with strangers	✓	
Chairing a meeting	✓	
Running meetings of any kind	✓	
Making a presentation	✓	
Speaking in front of a group	✓	

Now to assess the results.

There are four aspects to look at in evaluating this skills check-list. They are the following:

- your strongest area;
- the area you would like to improve in;
- your weakest area;
- skills you need in the future.

The word 'area' means the categories under which skills are grouped, eg training, leadership, interpersonal, etc.

Your strongest area

There are two things to look at here:

- the area where you have the most ticks in the 'Good' column;
- the area where you have the most ticks whichever column they appear in.

Weigh up where your strengths lie. You may be particularly strong in one area, or there may be three or four areas where you seem to be about the same. By assessing your strengths, you can target the areas where you want to improve.

The area you would like to improve in

Think carefully about this. You may want to choose an area where you have some degree of skill but you are hoping to improve considerably and excel. On the other hand, given that all these areas cover management skills, you may want to select an area where you did not have many ticks. To start with, it might be an idea to take steps to improve an area that will give you the most confidence.

But what about your weakest area?

Your weakest area

The important thing to remember here is that — whatever your weakest area — you can improve it if you want to.

For now, you may want to concentrate on a particular skill set and improve your weakest skills later. It may be that your weakest area is the one that you want to improve. That is fine.

At least you know the area where you are going to make the changes.

Finally — what about the future?

Skills you need in the future

Now you need to think carefully about your next job and what skills you might need. Some women find that they are acknowledged to be doing a first-class job at one level and yet keep being passed over for promotion. This means that the company is viewing them in a particular way and is not being given any reason to view them differently.

How are you viewed by your organisation? Are you seen as having the qualities that are needed at the next level? Look at the people who are getting promoted. What qualities do they have, and what skills are they offering? What weaknesses are you judged to have that might make someone think twice about promoting you?

Once you have identified the next job you want, analyse what skills you will need, and then demonstrate that you have them. If the job you want is in your present organisation, then you have to let your manager see your new skills.

Now that you have had a chance to assess your skills, qualities and knowledge, complete the chart below as a summary of your present skills and future plans.

Assessing myself

My strongest area/s:

Interpersonal
Planning + organisation.
Caring + information
training

I would like to improve in the area/s of:

assertiveness
communication
leadership
performance

My weakest area/s:

as above.

But I accept that I can change this/these if I want to.

Five skills I need for my next job:

People are often asked at interview, 'What can you offer this organisation?' This is rather a sneaky question but one that will certainly show up whether you have assessed your skills or not! Knowing your skills is one thing — telling someone else what they are is quite another!

Write a promotional presentation outlining your main strengths, qualities and skills, to answer the question, 'What can you offer this organisation?' Use all the exercises you've completed so far to help you and look at the model we have done in order that you can see the kinds of things to include.

What can you offer this organisation?

This example has been written by an area manager for a fast-food chain.

Opportunity offered & taken

In my previous job as a catering manager I had the opportunity of developing my managerial skills, holding direct responsibility for all aspects of running this particular type of outlet in terms of budgeting controls, people management and maintaining consistently high standards. In the process I succeeded in building a team spirit in my staff and enjoyed their loyalty and friendship.

Evidence of team leadership

Goal set & achieved

Through my 6 months as Head Chef in an Alpine hotel, I realised a lifelong ambition to work abroad and also achieved a high degree of professionalism in the practical culinary field, winning acclaim for my skills.

shows initiative

In my current job, I have become familiar with all aspects of franchising and am closely involved with the development of a new and rapidly expanding business idea. This has given me the opportunity to broaden my knowledge in many different areas of business: in marketing, I have assisted in the branding, image building, and targeting of a new concept; operationally, I have been personally involved in the setting up of operational systems for use across the franchise. I have also been involved in establishing the feasibility of the proposition offered to the franchisees and its viability once put into practice.

Keen involvement with new projects

Enthusiasm and motivation

In the training field I have developed and implemented training programmes and enjoy a great personal satisfaction from the successful results of these programmes. In maintaining the high standards in each unit, I have found my skills at negotiation and selling to be vital as they are of such great importance when dealing with franchisees.

Good organiser and time manager; works well under pressure

My current involvement in opening new stores calls on all my organisational, coordination and training skills, as the time between the builder's completion and the opening date is rarely more than two days.

Balanced lifestyle – a good antidote to the pressures of the job!

I have gained immense satisfaction from the rebuilding and decorating of my home, enjoy an active social life and love entertaining — practising my skills and new culinary ideas on my friends. I am a dedicated skier and a fair weather windsurfer, and I am a member of a health club whose gym and pool I try to use regularly.

What can you offer this organisation?

Now look back at the model to see if there is anything you have missed. Make changes if necessary. When you have finished, read it out to your family and/or friends. Do they realise how talented you are? Tape yourself reading your presentation and listen to how skilled you are. Practise it until you feel comfortable saying what you are good at. Not only will it remind you of all that you can do, but it will also help you when preparing for your next interview.

This is how one woman manager displayed her skills, qualities and knowledge.

Case study

Marketing manager for a large toy manufacturer.

'In order to demonstrate management potential, I had to show I knew a lot about the business we were in and also that I understood where the company wanted to be. To show I had views on the company's strategy, I put forward suggestions as to what it should be doing against its competitors and, in particular, made them relevant to the actual job I wanted. I had to show capability and confidence in myself and prove I could be professional.

The company was looking for a manager with new ideas, so I had to demonstrate initiative and get-up-and-go. If your employers tend to think younger people are more suited to promotion, then go back through your track record in previous positions and show you can make a contribution through your vast experience; but if you have formal qualifications, make the most of them. If you get the opportunity to take on more responsibility, then do so; if you don't, then ask for it, and make it as broad as possible. Once managers recognise your ability, they will probably throw more responsibilities at you. If managers, doubt whether a woman could do the job, demonstrate that you are capable and willing. It's important to be positive and convinced that the job would be right for you and to convey that attitude to the right person.

Now that you are aware of your own skills, qualities and knowledge, you should be feeling good about yourself — have more confidence in your own ability. The next section looks at confidence in more detail.

A Confident You

When people call someone 'confident', there seems to be general agreement about what is meant. Or is there? Is being confident to do with how you feel or how you act? Where does confidence come from? Are people born with it or do they learn it? Why are some people more confident than others? What sort of barriers act against confidence? Is it true that men are more confident that women? Is confidence always desirable? What do we mean by 'overconfident'?

This chapter looks at what is meant by confidence and gives you the chance to assess your own level of this quality. It also considers why confidence is such an important attribute for women preparing for a role in management. It then goes on to consider the three essential stages in developing confidence — accepting yourself, liking yourself and making the most of yourself.

WHAT IS CONFIDENCE?

To start with, assess the times when you feel confident.

Below are some of the times when women have said they feel confident. Tick which ones are true for you and add any of your own to the bottom of the list.

I feel confident when:

☐ I've had a good night's sleep.

- ☐ I'm spending money.
- ☑ I have my manager's backing.
- ☐ I'm busy.
- ☑ I have support from colleagues.
- ☑ I'm well dressed.
- ☑ I'm dressed appropriately for the occasion.
- ☑ I know what I'm talking about.
- ☑ I look good.
- ☐ I'm in a small group.
- ☐ I'm with friends.
- ☑ I'm in my own environment.
- ☑ Other people agree with me.
- ☑ I have prepared for a situation.
- ☐ I'm talking on the telephone.
- ☐ I'm working with other people.
- ☐ I've won something.
- ☑ I'm doing something I'm good at.
- ☑ I've got make-up on.
- ☑ Someone compliments me.
- ☑ Someone praises me.
- ☑ I know that someone likes me.
- ☑ I've done something successfully.
- ☑ I've had a drink.
- ☐ I'm on holiday.
- ☐ People are nice to me.
- ☑ I feel happy.
- ☑ I've achieved something.

I stand up for others.   ☐

I've got all the information I need.   ☐

☐

☐

☐

The examples used in that exercise cover the whole spectrum of situations — home, work, the way you look, and the way you feel. It is quite possible that the majority of the ones you ticked were from out-of-work situations. That is fine. The good thing about confidence is that it is a skill, and skills can be learned. They can also be transferred from one situation to another. Therefore skills associated with home life are equally applicable in the work environment. If you are brimming with confidence at home, the same should be true at work!

Here are some definitions of confidence which other women have given:

- Confidence is a feeling of well-being and self-worth.
- Confidence is believing in yourself and your abilities.
- Confidence is reflected in the way you think, the way you feel, and the way you appear to others.
- Confidence is 'an outer manifestation of inward self-esteem'.
- Confidence is when you know and like who you are.
- Confidence is being in control of yourself and any situation you are in.
- Confidence is accepting how you are instead of how others would like you to be.
- Confidence is being open with others and inspiring them to put their trust in you.
- Confidence is valuing yourself, believing in yourself, and standing up for yourself.

Do you agree?

Write down your definition of confidence. You may use, adapt or amalgamate any of the suggestions given above, or you may come up with your own.

```
Confidence is . . .




```

This is what you are aiming for — whatever your starting-point.

Is it so important for women to be confident? What is the connection between being confident and being successful?

Ten reasons for being more confident

1.   *The confident woman is in control of her life.* Confidence allows women to take initiatives, take risks, and be proactive instead of reactive. You can do this only if you feel in control of a situation. Being in control also means that you can choose what you do. This, in turn, increases confidence.

2.   *The confident woman is less likely to be victimised or manipulated.* Being confident means that messages are sent to others about how they may and may not treat you. How many times have you heard people say, 'I don't know why it's always me that ends up having to do it. So-and-so never gets asked.' Well, maybe that is because so-and-so would refuse if asked. Being confident is being able to state clearly what you want and how you feel.

3.   *The confident woman operates from strength — not weakness.* Of course, you can do this only if you know your own strengths. Many women are much more familiar with

their weaknesses. If you ask, 'What can't you do?' or 'What mistakes have you made?', most women could talk for hours. Sometimes the mistakes they refer to happened years ago, yet these are as clear in their minds as if it were yesterday.

If you ask, 'What are you good at?', many women say things such as 'I'm not too bad at ——', or 'I wouldn't exactly say I was good ——', or 'I'm fairly good at ——', or 'I could have a go at ——'. Try asking some of your female friends and colleagues what they are good at. Notice how many of them add qualifiers such as 'fairly' or 'quite', and how many of them laugh after they have said something they are good at, or immediately put themselves down — 'I'm good at delegating, but I'm sure it's only because I like telling other people what to do.'

4. *Confidence inspires respect.* If you are confident you give the impression of knowing what you are doing. The more positive you are, the more likely you are to be noticed and impress other people. This is different from seeking to please other people. People respond to those who are positive and confident. If you are not, others will assume the confident role in your place, and you will pass unnoticed. Any management position puts you in a position of authority, and you will need your confident image to establish yourself and inspire the respect of your colleagues.

5. *Confidence is the key to increased effectiveness at work.* Think of all the times when you have had a really good day at work. What made it good? Was it that you got a lot done? You were on top of what your were doing? Your boss was out and you had a free rein? Whatever the reasons, it is likely that confidence played a big part in it. Your self-confidence is a key aspect of your personality because it determines what you will and can do.

6. *Confidence is seen as the most important trait of a high performer.* If you are confident, people will trust you to handle whatever situation you are in. As you go up the career

ladder, you will encounter problems, difficult decisions and new situations that you will be expected to control. The people who appoint you to these positions have to be sure that you will not crumble under pressure. Negative feelings about yourself — 'I'll never handle that' and 'I'm dreading that meeting' — will be transmitted to others, and will affect the likelihood of your gaining promotion.

7. *Improved confidence leads to better communication with others.* Women have many strengths in the area of communication. Research shows that women are skilled in interpreting non-verbal communication. They are quick to see when communication lines are down, and quick to see distress in others. Improved confidence can also help verbal skills. Speaking confidently means making positive and assertive statements. This will enable you to tell people what you think and feel, while still respecting their rights. Others will not have to guess what you mean, or have to interpret clues you throw out to them. Confidence means you will be able to say the difficult things, and will not be destroyed by someone disagreeing with you or criticising you.

8. *Confident women are less likely to depend on others for approval.* If you value yourself, your abilities and your own worth, then approval from others is not so important any more. Of course, it is nice to be liked and thought of as doing a great job, but it is impossible to please all of the people all of the time, and it is not necessarily a good thing to try. Managers have to do a good job whether they are liked or not. Being dependent upon others' approval leads into the trap of doing only that which will please others. Confident women can be objective about the job they do because they operate from their strengths and value their own opinions.

9. *Confident women know where they are going — and how they can get there.* When asked about their jobs, women tend to look at the present, not where they will be in five or even ten years' time. Men, on the other hand, tend to have a clear direction — they know where they are

going and have set a clearly defined route.

A recent research project interviewed male and female managers, all at the same level in an organisation. The researchers spoke to the individuals concerned and then their managers. They said that performance was equally good, but the male managers were more confident than the female managers. The researchers went back three years later. Guess what? About 70 per cent of the male managers had moved on and up, while about 70 per cent of the female managers were still doing the same job. Lack of confidence is seen by organisations as having serious consequences for women's promotion chances, and self-confidence is the quality most often named by women as the one they would like.

10. *Positive thinking is conducive to health, happiness and success.* Now you have made a start. In Chapter 1 you looked at your own skills, qualities and knowledge which you can offer to an organisation. That is stage one. The next stage is to accept yourself for what you are and like yourself enough to believe in what you have to offer. Finally, present yourself in such a way that others believe in you too.

Confidence is all of the following:

1. Accepting yourself.

2. Liking yourself.

3. Making the most of yourself.

ACCEPTING YOURSELF

First of all, judge whether you really accept yourself.

In the list below, tick the characteristics which are true for you. You:

say 'That's just the way I am' about your behaviour traits; ☐

cannot sleep if something unpleasant has happened to you; ☐

☐ do things in a particular way because they have always been done that way;

☐ use 'if only' qualifiers, as in 'If only I hadn't said/done that';

☑ feel there are lots of things that you *should* do, even though you do not particularly want to do them;

☐ think 'It's not fair' about a lot of things;

☐ blame your manager/job/partner/circumstances/society for your feelings of misery;

☐ complain regularly about things that have happened to you;

☐ do not like being different from anyone else;

☑ wish you had someone else's looks or personality or job;

☐ think you should not do something if no one else is doing it;

☐ do not like to be the first to do or say something;

☐ give in if someone says, 'Why should you be an exception?'

☐ always need permission before you do something;

☐ say 'I'm sorry' a lot;

☐ smile when you are criticising others or when you are angry;

☐ think or say, 'What will people think?'

☐ worry or feel anxious if someone disagrees with you;

☐ put up with poor service or products rather than complain about them;

☐ say you agree with people and nod your head when you do not agree at all.

How did you get on?

The fewer the ticks, the more you have come to terms with yourself and taken one of the biggest steps towards increasing your confidence. The more ticks, the less you accept yourself.

You find it difficult to free yourself from the past, and you seek to please too readily. You also spend too much time comparing yourself to others.

If it is any consolation — the majority of women find it difficult to accept themselves. Some people think accepting yourself means accepting yourself as you are — faults and all. Implicit in this is the idea that people cannot change themselves. This is not the case. Accepting yourself goes much further than this. It means:

■ accepting that what has happened to you has made you the way you are.

But it also means:

■ choosing whether this is the way you really want to be;
■ recognising that you are a unique individual;
■ pleasing yourself rather than always trying to please others.

Look back at the boxes you ticked in the previous exercise and select three things you are going to *stop* doing in order to help you to accept yourself for the person you are.

1.

2.

3.

Once you accept yourself for what you are, you can move forward to liking yourself that little bit better.

LIKING YOURSELF

As with accepting themselves, many women find it difficult to like themselves.

How many times have you felt or said the following?

☐   I wish I was a better wife/mother/lover.

☐   I tried my best but I knew I couldn't finish on time.

☐   I am not bad at ——

☐   He said I couldn't do it, and now I know he was right.

☐   I would like more time to myself, but the family come first.

☐   I feel really selfish when I do something for *me*.

☐   I sometimes cannot sleep through worry.

☐   Do I look OK?

☐   I wish I were Superwoman.

☐   I would like to try, but I know I could not do it.

Once you have accepted yourself and your potential, it is easier to like yourself because you will have begun to free yourself from the past, stopped comparing yourself with others, and started doing what you want to instead of pleasing other people all the time.

Here are some guidelines to help you like yourself:

How to like yourself

- Spend some time on your own — getting to know yourself, your strengths and your wants.
- Stop making negative statements about yourself (see the list that follows — 'Negative statements I must stop making').
- Write down all the things you like about your appearance and your personality. Tell them to yourself in the mirror. Remember — if you like what you see then you are the person you should be.
- Stop blaming yourself for everything that goes wrong.
- Look after yourself at least as well as you look after others.
- Start agreeing with people who compliment you — or at least say a simple 'thank you'.
- Stop trying to understand everyone else all of the time.

- Look in the mirror every day and say, 'I like you — and I'm going to do something nice for you today'. Then make sure you do!
- Stop thinking about what you cannot do and start concentrating on what you can do.
- Do not use guilt to keep you in the past as a way of avoiding facing up to the future.
- Do not allow your feelings about the past to affect your actions in the present.
- Do not worry about things over which you have no control.
- Ask your friends to tell you what they like about you . . . and believe them.
- Tell yourself that if someone does not like you that is his or her problem — it does not mean you have to change.

Now for those negatives.

Negative statements I must stop making

When complimented:

- 'Oh, I've had this for years.'
- 'I got it in a sale.'
- 'You wouldn't believe how cheap it was.'
- 'To tell you the truth, it's not mine.'
- 'This colour of hair runs in the family.'
- 'It's kind of you to say so' (ie you and I both know you don't mean it).

When being praised:

- 'I only came in at the end.'
- 'I couldn't have done it without Mike's help.'
- 'I did the easy bit — they did all the hard work.'
- 'What are they after?'

When voicing opinions:

- 'My husband says . . .'
- 'My mother always told me . . .'
- 'I heard the other day that . . .'
- 'Isn't that right, dear?'
- 'Just ask Joan, she'll tell you.'

■   'That's just what I said, isn't it, Tom?'

If you can accept yourself and like yourself, your confidence
will grow.

MAKING THE MOST OF YOURSELF

If you feel confident, it is easy to project that confidence to
others, who will relate to you in a more positive way than if
you appear insecure and unsure. And in a management
position this positive reaction from others is vitally important.

However, whether you have inner confidence or not, there
are certain things you can do to appear more confident —
things which transmit external messages of self-assurance
while your inner thoughts and feelings are still learning to
catch up!

Here are seven steps you can take to appear more confident
— to make the most of yourself.

Make the most of yourself — step by step

Believe in yourself

Remind yourself of your strengths — the skills, qualities and
knowledge you identified earlier. If it helps, write them down
on a piece of paper and carry them round with you. In
moments of doubt you can then remind yourself what a skilled
individual you are. Remember that if you do not feel good
about yourself, then others are not likely to feel good about
you either. Believing in yourself makes others believe in you
too.

Make good use of eye contact

Of all the parts of the body which transmit information, the
eyes are the most powerful. Making and maintaining eye
contact helps people to appear more confident. It also improves
the ability to listen to what is being said — to listen and
understand.

Looking is much more than seeing — it also conveys
meaning. There is a virtually limitless number of signals that
can be transmitted by the eyes.

Looking away from people can give the impression that you are concealing something. It can make you appear bored or even slightly dishonest. On the other hand, to maintain eye contact all the time can make others feel uncomfortable. Staring at someone constantly can be quite intimidating.

There is, however, a happy medium. Maintain good eye contact and glance away occasionally. It is quite natural to break eye contact from time to time, particularly if you are deep in one-to-one conversation and need to concentrate on what to say next.

Adopt the correct expression

An inappropriate facial expression can undermine what you are trying to convey to the other person. This causes confusion in the mind of the receiver, particularly when you are complaining or giving and receiving criticism. Women, in particular, smile their way through the day — at managers, children, neighbours, or shop assistants — and while it could be argued that a friendly image is a confident image, a smile accompanying angry or unpleasant words confuses the receiver and detracts from the statement being made. It is hardly surprising that women sometimes are not taken as seriously as they should be.

When some women smile, they also tilt their heads to one side. This could convey the messages 'I am shy', or 'I am cute', or even 'I lack confidence'. Women often adopt this little-girl act without realising it. The danger in doing this is that it may make them appear uneasy in the presence of authority figures. If women behave as inferiors, it is little wonder they are sometimes treated as such.

Listen to your own voice

Avoid shrill tones and raising your voice at the end of phrases and sentences. However confident you look, you could ruin it as soon as you open your mouth. Lower your tone to sound more authoritative and do not speak too quickly. Speaking too loudly makes you sound aggressive, but speaking too quietly makes you appear unsure of what you are saying.

Control your body language

Be aware of how much you use your hands. A constantly wagging finger indicates aggression, while excessive movements of the hand may express nervousness. Avoid folding your arms in a figure-hugging, submissive way, or folding then in a matronly way, accompanied by a dominant stance and a glare. Many women stand with folded arms because they find it comfortable. However, the messages it sends — whether submissive or aggressive — are not good. You obviously can choose how you stand, sit and move, but you should be aware of what your non-verbal language is saying, and ask yourself if you wish to send those messages.

Think big

Standing straight and walking tall makes you look confident even if you do not feel confident! Hunched shoulders and a slouching posture give the impression that you are nervous and unsure of yourself. The other extreme, for example, walking purposefully into a room and looking straight ahead, can convey arrogance, even though you might enter a room that way because you dare not look at the eyes that will automatically turn your way! To feel comfortable and look confident, stand with your feet shoulder-width apart, and your shoulders and arms relaxed. When walking, walk smoothly and at a steady pace, and when entering a room, try to get into the habit of glancing round the room as you walk in.

Set your style

Finally, the best way to feel good about yourself is to know that you look good. You need to find a personal style which makes you feel and look good. Know what suits you and make sure you are dressed appropriately for the occasion.

Many women adopt a formal image when they move into a more senior job — perhaps choosing always to wear a dark suit. In your organisation's culture this formal style may be exactly right. Moreover, it may make you feel more professional when dressed this way. However, you must feel comfortable in your clothes. Looking uncomfortable in your clothes may give the impression that you are uncomfortable in your job. Women who have deliberately adopted a different style of dress as an experiment have been amazed at the effect.

The good news for women is that so many styles are acceptable in the work environment that you have virtually a free choice — as long as it is smart and comfortable. This means that women have a chance to break away from what they might see as a male tradition of acceptable dress, and choose a new image for themselves.

Your appearance is your first point of contact with other people. Do not lose the opportunity to present the image you want people to have of you — and make certain that confidence is a large part of it. The following is what one woman manager found when she changed her style.

Case study

Beryl Lymer has worked her way up through the ranks of the information technology division of a large company to become the managing director. She now heads a project team for 19 universities.

One year I invested a few hundred pounds in clothes and changed my image to fit in with the company dress code. People who were aware of my ability to do the job, and who had worked with me for years, actually thought I was working harder and doing things differently. They also thought I had changed, although the only thing that had changed was my clothes. I received my biggest pay rise that year, so it certainly had an impact!

Finally, here is a check-list you can use to help you make the most of yourself.

Check-list — confident me

Tick the boxes when you are confident you can:

recognise that the skills, qualities and knowledge you have are just as valuable as those of other people; ☐

maintain good eye contact and use it appropriately; ☐

- [ ] adopt the most suitable facial expression for the occasion;
- [ ] use the correct vocal tone and volume to get your point across;
- [ ] control your hands and arms so that you look neither aggressive nor submissive;
- [ ] stand straight and walk tall to present a poised and self-assured image;
- [ ] feel comfortable and confident with your personal style of dress and appearance.

Choosing a
Management Job

You have now assessed your own talents — skills, qualities and knowledge — and have a basis on which to build your confidence levels. It is now time to decide on the type of job you want and to match your talents to what is available. This chapter allows you to consider the area of management you would like to work in. It examines your personal work values, before moving on to formulate a career goal. It also looks at ways of finding a vacancy for a management post.

WHICH MANAGEMENT JOB?

In order to set a career goal, you need to consider what type of management job you would like and are suited to. There is a whole range of jobs which come under the umbrella of 'management'; they include:

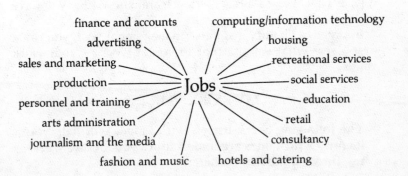

finance and accounts
advertising
sales and marketing
production
personnel and training
arts administration
journalism and the media
fashion and music

Jobs

computing/information technology
housing
recreational services
social services
education
retail
consultancy
hotels and catering

The list is by no means exhaustive, and there are lots of other fields where you may look for a management position. For an idea of the jobs on offer, you might like to use some of the following sources of information.

- training agency services and publications;
- your local careers office/jobcentre;
- your local library information service;
- any association to which you, or your organisation, may belong;
- women's networks;
- local and national newspapers.

The type of management post that you are looking for may be determined by the job that you are doing at present. You may enjoy it and wish to continue in the same line of work. You may have chosen a management field in line with your present qualifications, skills and experience.

However, if you want to transfer from your present field to something completely different, it is your professionalism and commitment which count. If you have the interest, enthusiasm and incentive to learn, many employers may well consider you, irrespective of your lack of experience in that specific area.

Be wary of confining your job search to management situations which are traditionally thought of as 'woman's domain', such as personnel and office administration. Although it may be easier to enter such a management job initially, you may find that salary, status and career prospects are not as good as you had hoped. There are opportunities for women in all types of careers. Therefore, keep an open mind and consider what you really want out of a new management role, as well as the skills, experience and knowledge you have to offer.

In order to identify a suitable management post, you must first assess what is important to you at work — your work values.

MY WORK VALUES

The following check-list of work values will help you identify which ones are important to you. Before working through the list, consider:

- the values which are important to you in your present job and which you would like to retain;
- the values which you may not have at present, but which you are looking for in a new career.

If there are others which are not included in the list, add them to the bottom.

Work values check-list

A high income ☐

Security ☐

A good pension ☐

Prospects for promotion ☐

Opportunities for travel ☐

Flexible hours ☐

Status ☐

Contact with a lot of people ☐

Job mobility ☐

Working in a small team ☐

Working alone ☐

Variety of tasks and activities ☐

Opportunity to write ☐

Chance to do research ☐

Work of social value ☐

Intellectual challenge ☐

Administrative work ☐

Working on more than one site/location ☐

Working with a predominantly young staff ☐

A competitive environment ☐

Working in your own community ☐

☐   Working under pressure
☐   Short working hours
☐   Opportunities for implementing creative ideas
☐   Recognition for a job well done
☐   Friendship and fun
☐   Opportunities for further training
☐   A female-orientated environment
☐   A pleasant (eg rural) location
☐   Working in a city
☐
☐
☐
☐
☐

It does not matter how many or how few you have ticked.
What does matter is that you look for these values in your new
career. The greater the correlation, the more rewarding the
job. If you have ticked a number of boxes, it is important to
prioritise these values in order that you know what is *most*
important to you in a new career.

**Choose the five values which are most important for
you, and list them below.**

My work values
1.
2.
3.
4.
5.

There are no right or wrong values when it comes to making a decision about the type of job that you want. You just need to be sure that the values are *yours*, not those of your partner, your best friend or your boss.

When you look for a job, try to select one where you can find expression for those values. For instance, if you have decided that it is important to work closely with others, then you will not be happy in a job where you have to spend long periods working on your own. If it is important that your work has social value, you may not be happy working in a fiercely competitive business environment.

Initially, it may be more important for you to get your foot in the door of management, rather than to concentrate on selecting the 'ideal job'. If this is the case, you may find it helpful to come back to this exercise as you move up the career ladder towards your ultimate goal in management.

MY CAREER GOAL

Once you know what you are looking for, you can select strategies that will lead you to your goal. Goals are important because they help in the planning process and provide direction. Successful people always have goals. After all, success is all about knowing what you want and going after it. Why, then, do some women find it difficult to set career goals?

- Some women are not used to setting long-term goals — thinking in terms of what they are going to be doing for the rest of their lives. The result is missed opportunities and that 'if only' feeling.
- Too often plans are made to accommodate other people. When there is a conflict between work and family, most women give priority to family needs, meaning that career goals take second place.
- Because of a lack of relevant skills a lot of women do not set high aspirations for themselves. They think in terms of the jobs they have always done, rather than looking at what they could do.
- Some women do not have the confidence to set their sights beyond their present capabilities.

■ Lack of support for their own career can cause some women to restrict their ambitions. Some men provide vocal support to the idea of equal career development, but are reluctant to commit themselves to action when it is a question of supporting their own partners. Employers, too, do not always give women the encouragement they need to aim high.

These are just some of the reasons why some women are not accustomed to the idea of setting a career goal. However, if you are aiming for a career in management, you must have a career goal. How will you know when you have arrived if you do not know where you are going in the first place?

Read the following case studies, which outline how two women managers arrived at their career goals.

Case studies

Anna Gilbert, Duty Operations Manager, Manchester Airport

I was basically a hopeless case as I didn't know where I wanted to go after leaving university. So I drifted into retailing. I moved to the airport after taking stock, when I was about 27 years old, and decided to change to the job I wanted. I then began to map a career to my present job — applying for posts which I knew would get me to where I am now.

I think it's important to direct your life instead of waiting for things to happen. I am now much more likely to set goals and define what I want from a job and from life in general. It's down to you to take the opportunities and keep 'bashing at the door' if there are barriers against women in the organisation.

Christina Ezard, Branch Manager, Barclays Bank, Stockport

When I started in the bank in the seventies I began to question why all these men were being promoted over me, because I thought I was doing a good job. When I realised that I needed qualifications I found it was uncommon for women to take banking exams. Despite this, I went ahead. I set about working very hard to ensure I passed the examinations and achieved the goals I set for myself. Over the next three or four years my career began to take off. It's important to be assertive in certain situations to ensure you achieve your goals.

Now write down your career goal. Try to be as specific as possible.

My career goal

If you were able to identify a goal, you now know what you are working towards. If not, give it a little more thought and come back to the exercise when you are ready. Do not leave it too long, though. When you reach the interview stage you may be asked what your career plans are. Even if you are keeping yourself open to new opportunities, make sure that this does not become an excuse for drifting. Take control and decide what you want from a career.

Identifying your goal does not mean that you cannot change your mind. You need to retain a certain amount of flexibility in order to take advantage of new opportunities, and to take account of any changes to your circumstances and values. You will need to reappraise your goal from time to time, in order to know when it is time to move to another job. As your career develops and you gain in confidence and ability, your goal may change.

Take some time to review your goal and modify it, if necessary. Achieving what you want is possible — if you plan. Success, whether in management or in anything else, is not simply luck. Luck is where preparation meets opportunity — and it is up to you to take those opportunities when they present themselves.

Now that you have assessed your work values and have

considered your career goal, it is time to find out what is on offer.

FINDING A VACANCY

One of the most common methods of finding a vacancy is to scan the jobs columns in the national, trade and local press. A less common approach but one which can have excellent results is to find your own job.

Job adverts: reading between the lines

Most people rely on adverts in national newspapers and trade papers for professional posts. This is a good source of management jobs, but when trying to find the right job for yourself, make sure you read between the lines. This means that you have to ask yourself the following three questions:

1.   'Is this what I really want?'

2.   'Do I match the job description?'

3.   'Are there any new opportunities here for me?'

Is this what I really want?

Read the extracts from job adverts and circle the ones which appeal to you most.

IS THIS WHAT I REALLY WANT?

Many of our assignments are for full time standard employment but increasingly our clients are thinking <u>outside the square.</u>

will be part of a small team working on a busy factory site.

● Pairs of people wishing to Job share

– we would prefer to hear from two people, perhaps two qualified people, who can decide between themselves how to share a job.

two dynamic and conscientious people are required to form part of the Management team at this Regional Centre, which boasts a superb 33.3 metre main pool, diving and learner pools, a 2 court main hall, projectile hall, weights room, 6 squash courts, large ancillary hall and health suites and several other excellent facilities.

● Individuals who have specific time demands upon them making the standard 9 to 5 impossible, particularly accountants.

and the added bonus of living in one of the most attractive parts of rural Britain.

up to £20,000 + car, profit share and excellent benefits

you will have more personal control of your work, you will realise that together with the authority goes responsibility and accountability in terms of quality, time and cost. As a member of a small, young and hardworking team you will also have the talent to be responsible for an ever increasing project load and your consequent career development.

You will thrive under pressure, cheerfully, and be able to communicate effectively at all levels – in an environment with a remarkably young employee profile.

The Council operates a scheme for flexible working hours and applications from job sharers are welcomed.

flexibility to allow for extensive overseas travel will be essential.

our need is for self-confident, experienced consultants who enjoy the consultancy challenge, and are able to live away from home each week to join us.

— work independently within agreed guidelines
— collate and evaluate data and prepare reports
— relate to people at all levels, individually and in groups

your role will include attracting advertisers, liaising with printers, working closely with the Editor. Option of working from home.

The chance to show your initiative and flair in an authority which has a reputation for progressive thinking
● A spring board for further career development to a top managerial level
● Conditions of service which are second to none
● Above all, job satisfaction of the highest order in managing a facility of top quality

Work place NURSERY available

Probably single and certainly willing to travel, you want a highly rewarding and satisfying position specialising in recruitment. You must be able to establish professional credibility with senior managers in an aggressive fast-moving environment and establish working relationships at all levels.

In return, as well as an excellent salary we can offer you a substantial rewards package including large company benefits such as a bonus, two lease cars and a generous relocation allowance.

If these jobs were all suitable for you in most respects, there are some which would appeal in certain respects to you more than other jobs. What was the basis of your decision? Was it salary, hours, tasks involved or gut feeling? What it should have been based on is the work values you highlighted earlier.

Check your completed 'work values' list and see if the ones you have circled are consistent with what you said is important to you. If so, fine. If not, you might wish to revise your list of values.

'Is this what I really want?' is something that you need to consider for yourself, every time that you read a job description in the newspaper. There is a wide range of benefits associated with management jobs, and there are as many different benefits as there are jobs. It is up to you to find the right job for you.

The second question is:

Do I match the job description?

In order to match your experience and abilities to the requirements of the organisation, you need to go back to the exercises you completed in Chapter 1. Ask yourself what an organisation is really looking for, and then match your skills and experience to its requirements.

Here are some extracts from job ads for management posts. Read each one carefully, asking yourself, 'Do I match the job description?'

Do I match the job description?

Preferred age 35-45. Those at present earning less than £14,000 are unlikely to be qualified for this post.

Personal commitment and drive are essential, together with the ability to think laterally and develop imaginative cost effective marketing strategies.

Merchandising flair and the ability to motivate both your team and yourself are essential. If you enjoy working under pressure to the highest standards and have a proven track record in selling, you may be interested in what we have to offer.

It is anticipated that successful candidates will be aged between 22-30 years and will be willing to relocate for career progression. In return, they will be offered an attractive salary and other large company benefits combined with the opportunity to develop an exciting career.

Our client does not care what your experience is. Educational qualifications are not as important as being able to demonstrate effective man-management skills, and organisational ability.

You should be able to relate to staff at all levels and functions and preferably have had broadly based experienced in working in a number of different areas. Direct experience in working in a multiple retailing environment would be a distinct advantage.

You will need to have at least two years experience of advising people face-to-face, and the ability to supervise staff. Paid or unpaid work three days a week or more will be taken into account.

Man management skills and empathy are essential to maintain high morale and continue the spirit of dedication and loyalty which sums up the company's outlook.

In addition to which, we place considerable emphasis on self assurance, profit awareness and the ability to take decisions confidently within an environment which has all the pressures of a very rapidly expanding volume of business.

Afro-Caribbean, Asian and people of African origin are currently under-represented in the workforce. We therefore positively encourage applications from these communities.

He or she will be expected to control, motivate and lead a team of enthusiastic and competent Agency Sales Executives. He/she should enjoy detail work and be happy in working with facts and figures and be able to use original thought in presenting data in interesting ways.

To develop and to undertake an active role in the development of on-site staff communications, the company is looking for an experienced person with proven communications skills and expertise in local community relations. The role requires someone with the ability to listen as well as communicate.

Handwritten annotations:

- not definite
- potential for creative input here
- Can you cope with the demands of this job?
- Here's your chance!
- Do your varied experiences equip you for this job?
- are you a good communicator?
- New managers please apply
- is your commitment strong enough
- is this a challenge or a threat?
- an opportunity for you?
- Do you have this type of experience?

Do I match the job description?

In order to attract the right individuals, our Client is open-minded about the details of your track record. Nevertheless, it does need to be impressive – as do your communication and motivating skills.

We are seeking a mature and experienced marketing manager, who should ideally be familiar with current packaging and promotion techniques, understand the fmcg market, have a proven record of successful product development and innovativeness.

(your jargon, too!)

Successful applicants will probably:–

(but not necessarily?)

- have at least 5 years experience in preferably a commercial or industrial environment
- live within easy travelling distance of London
- be prepared to travel and work away from home
- have proven ability and experience in at least two of the course subject areas
- be able to speak to groups clearly and confidently

(very specific requirements)

you must have energy and enthusiasm, plus the willingness to take on real responsibility within a close-knit team.

(Essential management qualities)

– The successful candidate will have:–

- a general knowledge of markets, i.e. equities, options, commodities, futures and foreign exchange, and an in depth experience in at least one of these areas;
- maturity and the ability to successfully negotiate at a high level;
- proven ability to work with and motivate people;
- a character trait that leans strongly towards detail and precise accuracy;
- the temperament and flexibility for extensive international travel.

Do you get a kick out of setting goals and measuring the results of your efforts?

(Ever set any personal or team goals?)

As part of a small team shaping personnel policies throughout the District, your responsibilities will range over such varied management training areas as budgetary control, planning, time management and equal opportunity

(Can you transfer these skills from home to work?)

Our training scheme, based in one of our main branches throughout the UK and lasting about 12 months, will give you an excellent opportunity to familiarise yourself throughly with every aspect of our business. After satisfactory completion of this training comes a move to a Supervisory position. Further promotion, based on ability and performance, leads to Branch Management. Mobility is, of course, essential. In order to take advantage of promotion opportunities.

(We'll train you well, but:...)

Could you:
- head a large team of skilled staff in developing new community based services
- manage a residential training resource
- motivate staff working at the leading edge of mental handicap services
- create a service that meets multi-cultural needs
- communicate effectively with people with a mental handicap, parents and community resources
- encourage new involvement in developing the services
- set up professional planning and maintaining systems
- inspire confidence and trust in the service you advocate
- work as part of a multi-disciplinary management team

(does this rule you out?)

(Do you have this type of community experience?)

ability to work long, hard and irregular hours, and be capable of leading a group of highly committed staff. He/she will, by definition, be a dynamic and self-??????? individual.

This person should be a good organiser and should have proven ability to get results either as part of or through a team of people. Professionalism, flair and creativity will rate highly among our selection criteria.

(Sounds like a slog?)

(Are you a good team worker? And do you have lots of new ideas?)

(is this the language you understand?)

If you circled a number of adverts, good. It means you have the skills and experience that many organisations are looking for. If you circled a few, or even none, do not worry. The wording of many adverts is often deliberately vague because the organisations themselves have not decided exactly what they want from an applicant. Also many of them are couched in business terminology. When you work through the maze of jargon, you may well find that the skills sought are the skills you have.

Employers do not always expect the candidates for the job to be able to meet all the specifications they describe. They would like such multitalented people to apply, but they know that the supply of management jobs available outstrips the number of suitably qualified applicants.

So, even if you do not feel that you meet the description fully, yet still would like to apply for the job, go ahead and apply. Emphasise in your CV and at your interview how your skills and experience in other aspects of the job make you an ideal candidate for the post. As long as you are able to convince the interviewers that you are keen to develop new skills, willing to undergo further training, and quick to learn, you should have a good chance.

The third question to ask yourself when reading job adverts is:

Are there any new opportunities here for me?

If an organisation is undergoing change of any kind, it may be a good opportunity for more women to enter management. The organisation may be looking for a new approach which you can offer. A different style of management, a new perspective on old problems, a more balanced hierarchy — these are all reasons why an organisation might like to see more women in its management ranks.

What should you look out for? On the following job adverts, note particularly the words and phrases which are ringed. They indicate that there is an opportunity to show that you have something new to offer the organisation.

New opportunities

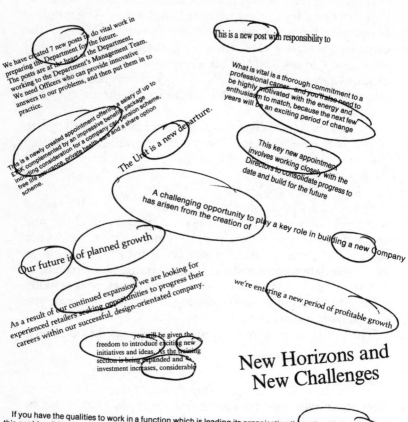

We have created 7 new posts to do vital work in preparing the Department for the future. The posts are at the heart of the Department, working to the Department's Management Team. We need Officers who can provide innovative answers to our problems, and then put them in to practice.

This is a newly created appointment offering a salary of up to £75K complemented by an impressive benefits package including consideration for a company car, pension scheme, free life assurance, private health care and a share option scheme.

The Unit is a new departure.

This is a new post with responsibility to

What is vital is a thorough commitment to a professional career and you'll also need to be highly motivated with the energy and enthusiasm to match, because the next few years will be an exciting period of change

This key new appointment involves working closely with the Directors to consolidate progress to date and build for the future

A challenging opportunity to play a key role in building a new Company

Our future is of planned growth

As a result of our continued expansion we are looking for experienced retailers seeking opportunities to progress their careers within our successful, design-orientated company.

we're entering a new period of profitable growth

you will be given the freedom to introduce exciting new initiatives and ideas. As the training section is being expanded and investment increases, considerable

New Horizons and New Challenges

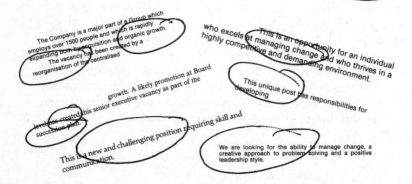

If you have the qualities to work in a function which is leading its organisation through radical change then this could well be the most exciting move of your career.

The Company is a major part of a Group which employs over 1500 people and which is rapidly expanding both by acquisition and organic growth. The vacancy has been created by a reorganisation of the centralised

who excels at managing change and who thrives in a highly competitive and demanding environment.

This is an opportunity for an individual

This unique post has responsibilities for developing

growth. A likely promotion at Board has created this senior executive vacancy as part of the succession plan.

This is a new and challenging position requiring skill and communication.

We are looking for the ability to manage change, a creative approach to problem-solving and a positive leadership style.

Finally, here are ten top tips to remember when reading job advertisements.

Top ten tips

1. Do not worry if you do not meet the job specification exactly. Very few applicants do. Aim to meet about two-thirds of the requirements.

2. An advertisement which specifies people aged around 30 means 26–37, but why should being 25 or 45 stop you from applying — if you really want the job?

3. Do not be discouraged by words such as 'ideally', 'probably' or 'likely'. Such words mean the organisation has not ruled out the possibility of accepting someone who does not meet these characteristics. If it is 'open-minded' in this way, use this as an opportunity to show what you can do for the organisation.

4. If the salary seems far above what you are getting at present, do not let this stop you from applying. Organisations are aware of the fact that many people are underpaid for what they do.

5. If the salary is on a par with, or even less than, what you are getting at present, do not let this put you off either, if it is a job you really want. Be prepared to convince the job selectors of your reason for wanting to make such a move. For example, it may be an opportunity to diversify your skills, or perhaps the organisation offers better prospects for promotion or training.

6. Vague advertisements which dangle five-figure salaries are probably on the rough end of selling and mainly commission-based.

7. Advertisements that are full of management jargon are probably aimed at people who talk the same language.

8. Do not be deterred by titles such as 'assistant'. An assistant in one firm may have more responsibility and salary than a manager in another.

9.   Do not be too hasty in rejecting job advertisements because of some preconceptions that you have about the organisation. You should be applying for vacancies which match your particular needs and qualifications.

10. If the advertisement does not provide as much information as you need, do not hesitate to ring or write for more.

If you scan the job pages fruitlessly, there is another method of getting the job you want in management — by finding or creating your own.

Finding your own job

Job ads are one way of getting yourself a job, but not the only way, and not necessarily the most successful. A large percentage of job seekers are able to find a job they want by other methods, and three of the most common methods are the following:

1. Creating a job.

2. Making a speculative application.

3. Using contacts.

Creating a job

Do not discount the possibility of creating a job for yourself where none exists at the moment. Within your present organisation you may be able to highlight an opportunity for creating a new management post. This may be the case if the organisation is going though a period of change, growth, merger, reorganisation, even recession.

Here is a case study of a woman who created her own job:

Case study: Frances

Frances was working in an administrative role for a management consultancy which had expanded quickly during the five years since it had started. She had been there from the beginning and done a variety of tasks which she had enjoyed.

As part of her job, she had handled enquiries from clients about the services that the company had to offer, and she believed that there was a market for putting some of these services into products. The partners who owned the consultancy were overstretched in carrying out their own respective tasks, and Frances saw this as an opportunity to diversify her own role by creating a new one.

Frances asked for an opportunity to discuss her work performance with her managers at their next monthly meeting, and she used this as an opportunity to present her ideas. She pointed out the skills that she had which she did not feel were being used at present, and suggested to the consultants how she and they could both benefit if she was given an opportunity to extend her role and improve their business prospects.

After considering her ideas in some detail and discussing some amendments to them, management agreed that Frances could implement some of her proposals, as long as she continued to do some of her previous tasks. This was a little disappointing for Frances, as she hoped that a newly appointed member of staff might be able to take over most of them, but she accepted the offer anyway.

In fact, this made her even more determined to succeed in her new role in order to jettison some of these other responsibilities. It was decided to review her progress regularly, and then to consider her future position in six months' time.

The enterprise was a great success. After a couple of early disappointments, which were due to lack of experience, her performance gradually improved. It was decided that 'product development manager' should be her new job title in the company. Frances has no regrets and loves every minute of it. 'I took a risk', she says, 'but it paid off. 'I'd never have considered doing this sort of thing at one time, but I felt that I was in a good position to create my own opportunity. I had nothing to lose by making the suggestion — and a lot to gain. It's given me a lot of confidence and trust in my judgement that I didn't have before.'

The moral of this case study is — that you should look for opportunities wherever you are. If your organisation is undergoing change of any description, there may be a chance for you to show how you can contribute in a positive way.

If you are looking for a job and select a small or rapidly expanding organisation, you may attract the attention of somebody who would be willing to create a job for you. Moreover, if you are the first one in this role, you have the potential to make of it what you will. The opportunities are there for you to make things happen.

A second method of finding your own job is to make a speculative application.

Making a speculative application

This is another way of finding a vacancy before it is advertised in the press.

Case study: Anne

Anne's first effort to find a management job resulted in 30 rejections and three interviews, but no job. So she changed tactics. She sent out copies of her CV with a personal letter to all the companies in her town which interested her.

One of her applications happened to land on the desk of the managing director of a tour company, who noticed from her CV that, although she did not have any experience of the world of travel, she had worked in the overseas department of a bank. The MD also recognised that languages were one of her strengths. A brief letter invited her for an informal interview, and after that she was invited back for further talks.

The result was that she was given a management post in the company's European travel department. The managing director said that he decided to see Anne because her CV was better presented than the ones he usually saw, and because she seemed to have the right combination of experience and skills that his company needed. 'I had nothing specific in mind when I met her,' he said, 'but a job evolved through discussion with other members of the board.'

The moral of this is that you should not wait for vacancies to land in your lap. Speculative applications can be very successful. They demonstrate that you have initiative, enterprise and interest. You may even be lucky enough to find that your letter arrives at the same time as a resignation in the company, and you save the personnel department the trouble and expense of filling the vacancy by other methods.

There are certain guidelines to follow if you want to find a job in this way.

How to make a speculative application

1. Make a list of the organisations in your area that you would like to work for. Use the Yellow Pages or trade directories in your local library.

2. Look in the local press for details of new companies who may be moving into the area, expanding organisations, and those undergoing some kind of change.

3. Ensure that your letter is specifically directed at the organisation you are applying to.

4. Ask yourself what you can offer — the combination of experience, knowledge and skills that a firm may need.

5. Send your CV and a covering letter which explains briefly and concisely why you are writing. Ask for an informal interview.

6. Consider a reason why you would like to work for this particular company and include this in your letter.

7. Identify the person in the organisation with the power to hire you and address the letter to this person. Ring the organisation and ask for the name of the senior personnel officer, or whoever is in charge of management recruitment.

8. Provide details about your availability — both for interview and for when you could start work.

9. Photocopy the letter and the CV as a record of what you said to each company!

    The third method of finding your own job is to use the people you already know.

Using contacts

You may be able to find a management post through somebody you know — a relative, friend or colleague who works in an organisation where you would like to be employed. Through these people you can learn of job vacancies and job opportunities — some of which may never be advertised. You can also find out about the organisation in depth, before submitting your application.

Another way to make contacts is to join a network. More and more professional women are doing this. It is a way of doing what men have always done through the old boy network, but this time it is 'women only'. Women need access to information if they are to move forward in their careers. But the opportunities to join the networks that men belong to may be restricted — if much of the networking takes place in the Gents, for instance! It is useful for women managers to have their own forum for meeting one another. And it is even more necessary for women who are in the minority as managers within their own organisation. This can lead to problems of isolation and diminishing confidence, particularly if the women concerned feel that they lack support from within the organisation.

A network enables professional women to get together with other like-minded women to offer mutual support. It is also a way of furthering business interests, and it may enable you to make contacts who can help you in various ways. A network helps by:

- telling you of vacancies as — or before — they arise;
- giving you contacts in an organisation who could give you advice or information on forthcoming posts;
- introducing you to people who may be interested in employing you;
- sharing ideas and information;
- providing support and encouragement to progress in your career.

If you come into contact with people who themselves have changed jobs recently, they may be able to give you useful advice on a successful approach to take. You may find that there is a network which is associated with your own

organisation or career. Try to make a few enquiries.
Why not start now?

**Make a list of all the people you know in organisation
networks or professional associations who might be able
to keep you abreast of any forthcoming posts. Consider
everybody you know — family, friends, neighbours,
colleagues (past and present), and acquaintances.**

My personal contact list

1.

2.

3.

4.

5.

6.

7.

8.

9.

10.

11.

12.

If you have managed to come up with some names, tell these
people what your requirements are, and how they can help
you. Make sure that you follow them up from time to time.

If you have not been able to identify any contacts at this
stage, do not panic. You may not know of anybody at the
moment, but, as you meet people in your present job, find out
exactly what they do. They may be able to help you in the
future. They may be able to offer advice and information on
the best approach to take, or the people to contact. Most people
will be willing to help — but they need to know that you are
looking. As you come across such people, add their names (and

any further useful information) to your personal contact list.
Whichever method you use for finding a vacancy, you still
need to submit an application, and this is the topic of Chapter 4.

4
Be Prepared

When you apply for a job, you are usually asked to complete an application form or submit a curriculum vitae (CV). In addition, you may also need to send in a covering letter. In this chapter you will find out how to plan an application for the job that you want and how to prepare for the job interview.

THE APPLICATION

The first step is to prepare your CV.

The curriculum vitae

When an attractive job is advertised, recruiters often get well over 100 replies. Some organisations get even more. This means that somebody has to wade through stacks of CVs. You do not want that somebody to dismiss your application without considering your qualifications, because there is something wrong with the presentation or format of your CV. 'Curriculum vitae' is a Latin phrase which means 'course of life'. It could also be described as your 'life history', as its purpose is to record all significant information about you for the attention of a prospective employer. Because it is a unique opportunity to 'sell yourself' on paper, it is worth putting time and effort into creating a first-class document.

Even if you are not asked to send a CV, the effort will not be wasted, as you will need the same information for completing an application form. When completed, the CV will be your own personnel record, which you can then modify and update, as necessary.

Here is a model CV:

Curriculum Vitae: Margaret Ann FREEMAN

Telephone

Home 0739 4332
Work 0739 7660 (ext 43)

Home Address

53 Waterloo Terrace
Norwich
East Anglia NW2 6RX

Date of Birth   30 August 1956

SUMMARY

At present I am employed as Personnel and Training Manager for a large contract catering company where I am involved in all aspects of Industrial Relations, on a local and national level. I was previously employed by a national distribution company where I was Computer Development Project Leader.

EMPLOYMENT

1985–Present

Personnel and Training Manager,
Bloggs (UK) Ltd — Contract Caterer

Key Responsibilities

- Recruitment and selection of management

- Training and management development

- Employee and industrial relations

- Project work — particularly in development areas and organisational design.

- Selling

1980–1985

Computer Development Project Leader,
Hurricane Express (Parcel Carrier)

Key Responsibilities

- Implementing a computerised operational system to be used throughout the company

---

- Data processing
- Scheduling and controlling the work of a team of four people

1978–1980

Office Manager
White Knight Insurance Company

Key Responsibilities

- Coordinating the work of the eight people in the department
- Budget control and all financial records
- Producing monthly financial reports

Other employment

During my vacations at college I worked as a freelance market research interviewer, where I was required to conduct an interview according to a prearranged schedule.

EDUCATION

1975–1978 Whiztown Polytechnic
BA (Hons) Combined Arts
English/History/Computer Studies
Class: 2.1

1967–1974 True Grit High School
8 O levels
3 A levels — English, German, History
RSA certificate in shorthand and typing

PRESENT INTERESTS

- Active member of local amateur dramatics company
- Representative on local committee for sports and recreation facilities
- Travel and meeting people

OTHER INFORMATION

Status — Single
Holder of a current driver's licence

There is no standard model of a CV, and thus there are a number of variations on the one shown here. However, this particular format is

- concise;
- clearly laid out;
- easy to read;
- informative.

Here are the guidelines that were used to write this CV, in terms of assembling and presenting the details.

Assembling the details — step by step

These are the details that should be included, in the following order:

1. Full name with surname in capitals.

2. Home address and postcode, and telephone numbers at home and at work (if possible).

3. Date of birth.

4. A summary of present and previous posts.

5. Employment details, starting with your present post. Provide details of skills and responsibilities. If you have had many jobs at the start of your career but two good jobs in the last five years, concentrate on those. Your last two jobs will be of most interest to a prospective employer.

6. Educational background — secondary school, college, university or other institutions, including dates.

7. Qualifications — giving the years they were obtained and from where. If your educational record is not very good, do not dwell on it. Focus instead on skills you have learned since leaving school.

8. Other interests and activities. Include only interests which are relevant to the job, for example, special skills such as languages, or membership of teams or clubs.

9. Other relevant information. This could include details of courses you have attended or are taking at present, other qualifications you have, talks you have given,

publications you have written, and whether you hold a driving licence. Avoid including any information which is not relevant to the job. For instance, it is not necessary to state the number of children that you have. Try to include all relevant information, but, at the same time, resist the temptation to write too much. Two or three pages are sufficient.

Once you have all the information, you can start to present it on paper.

Presenting the information on a CV — dos and don'ts

DO use good-quality, A4-size white paper.

DON'T put in anything negative — such as saying what you *cannot* do. Errors of omission are very hard to spot.

DO get it typed, if possible. If not, write in black ink. A typed CV looks more professional, and is usually easier to read.

DON'T say how much you are earning at present, unless specifically asked.

DO use bullets for lists.

DON'T cram everything on one page — use plenty of white space.

DO check! check! check! — proofread at least twice, to ensure there are no grammatical, punctuation or spelling errors. Finally, photocopy the completed document and keep the copy for your own reference.

Now you are ready to prepare your own CV.

Adapt your present CV, or write one for the first time, in accordance with the guidelines and model.

You will need information from the previous chapters to do this:

- skills check-list;
- assessing myself;
- what you can offer to this organisation;
- details of experience, qualifications and relevant dates.

CURRICULUM VITAE

CURRICULUM VITAE (continued)

Check that you have included all the information outlined in the step-by-step guidelines. When you are satisfied with your CV, you can use this one as a basis to adapt when you apply for specific jobs. Although much of the information will be standard to any CV you send out, you will need to modify it to take account of the particular requirements of the job. This is where it helps to do some research on the organisation before you complete your CV.

Get hold of the organisation's annual report. Ask questions of those who know something about the organisation. This way you can tailor your CV to suit the requirements. It is not a good idea to produce a CV in bulk. These can usually be spotted quite easily.

Remember — a skilfully written CV will not guarantee you the job, but it might get you an interview, in which case the time taken to prepare it will have been well spent!

Once you have prepared your CV, there is nothing so annoying as to find that you have to fill in an application form — particularly when it means that you have to provide all the same information as on your CV, but in half the space.

The application form

When you receive the job application you will probably also be given a job description which outlines all the main responsibilities of the job. This is an important piece of information which you should analyse carefully before starting to fill in the application form.

Look back to your own skills and experiences and match them to the requirements of the job. This will enable you to highlight the particular aspects of your career in which the organisation will be interested. Use your research on the organisation to indicate how you could make a valuable contribution. You do not need to go into too much detail, as you will be given an opportunity to expand on what you have said, if offered an interview.

Remember — you will be able to use your CV as a basis to work on when completing the application, as much of the information contained in the CV will be requested. All the guidelines about writing a CV apply to application forms, and there are some additional steps to remember.

How to complete an application form — step by step

1. Photocopy and save the original application form. Use the photocopy to write a first draft.

2. Read the form thoroughly, referring to the job advertisement as you read.

3. Complete each section in sequence.

4. Unless you are asked to write them in your own handwriting, type the details. If necessary, have the material typed professionally.

5. Be positive. Do not imply, 'I am fed up with my present job', but, rather, 'I am seeking new opportunities'.

6. In the section asking for any other information, emphasise the skills you have which are relevant to the job and the organisation. If you need more space, attach a separate sheet of paper. Write 'continued on enclosed sheet' on the application, and your full name and 'Continuation Sheet No. 1' on the sheet.

7. If you are asked to complete an application form, your CV will not be accepted as a substitute. But you could submit it with the application if you feel that it contains other information relevant to the post, or that it is particularly well-presented.

8. Do not bluff or lie. As a result of falsification, you may come unstuck in an interview.

9. Photocopy your completed job application, remembering to keep a copy and also the advertisement you replied to (including the name and date of the paper). You will need to reread them both carefully before going to an interview.

10. If you are asked for referees, choose them appropriately. They may vary, according to the nature of the job. Remember to ask their permission, and give them details of the job you are applying for, plus a copy of the application form. Your prospective employer may well telephone them for a verbal reference, and thus it

will enhance your prospects if your referees are well prepared too.

Finally, to accompany the CV, and perhaps the application form, you need to write a covering letter.

The covering letter

The covering letter will vary, according to whether it accompanies an application form or a CV. For an application form, you need only a brief covering letter, addressed to the relevant person (see job advertisement or additional information you received with the application). It should include the following information:

- the post for which you are applying;
- how you heard about it;
- the fact that you are enclosing a completed application form.

In the case of a curriculum vitae, the CV is the skeleton of your application; the covering letter is the flesh. The latter gives a 'sense of you'. It gives you a greater opportunity to tailor your application to suit a particular job.

Here is a check-list to use when writing a covering letter for a CV application.

Check-list — a covering letter

☐ The letter is typed or written in black ink.

☐ Writing paper is white and unlined.

☐ It covers no more than one sheet of paper.

☐ It is addressed to the individual named in the advert, for example, 'Dear Mrs Smith'; and it closes with 'Yours sincerely'. If no name is given, use 'Dear Sir or Madam' and close with 'Yours faithfully'.

☐ The covering letter mentions where you saw the advert, and gives a thoughtful reason why the job appeals to you, and why you think you should be considered.

A concise summary of your key skills is included, as they apply to the requirements of the job. □

You show the prospective employer how you can meet the company's requirements. You will get a chance to expand on this at the interview — but if you do not make an impression at this point, you will never get that far. □

You send off the CV/application form/covering letter (as required) in an A4 envelope, by first-class post. □

The importance of getting the application right is evident from the small number of candidates who reach the interview stage. When checking your application for the last time before you pop it into the envelope, ask yourself:

'Would I employ *me*?'

The answer should be *'Yes'*.

As you are well aware, however laborious the task of applying for the job, it is nowhere as gruelling as the next stage — the interview. You are going to prepare for that now.

THE INTERVIEW

The final crucial stage of the job search is the interview. It is a nerve-racking process for everyone who applies for a new job. Feeling slightly nervous is actually very positive — the adrenalin is flowing and you are on your toes. Feeling too nervous, however, has the opposite effect. This part considers how you can be well prepared and cope with the questions on the big day itself. It also looks at how to cope with disappointment.

The following case studies show how four women prepared for interview for management posts. The first example is the preparation for a senior management post; the others are for general managerial roles.

Case studies

Beryl Lymer, Project Manager, Information Technology, for 19 universities throughout the UK

I spent two days on preparation to get my present job. On the first day I revised all the relevant literature I possessed. This involved spending time looking at people management as well as the project management side. I made notes on each subject and wrote out my approach to the job, project and people. I didn't intend to give these notes to the interview panel but in the end I did, which left a lasting impression on them.

On day two I went to a friend's computer agency which deals with the software used in the job I was applying for. I talked to people about the system and gained access to some books. This meant I could talk sensibly about the system although I was not an expert on it. It helped me to psyche myself up so I was prepared.

It worked well — I'd done my homework and got the chance to put my points across. I also got the job!

A senior airport manager

I feel that one of the most important elements of being successful in an interview is to make sure that you do your homework about the company you are applying to. You have to do what you can to stand out from the rest. Companies are looking for people who have an interest in what they do and the way they operate.

It's also important to have some questions ready — managers have to be questioners. So carry out some background research before attending the interview. Get hold of the latest company report, read the local newspapers for references — in fact anything you can.

Mo Bradford, Associate Manager of the Institute of Consumer Ergonomics at Loughborough University

I believe that preparation is an essential factor before an interview. I would start by making a list and then apply the 3 Ps — Plan it; Prepare it; Practise it. Think about making a list of the points you want to raise and perhaps even undertake a role-play situation with a friend.

When you're actually in the interview, emphasise that your own style is not better but different and bring out those differences you can offer as a woman. It's also a good idea to get organised and make a set of your own notes that you don't mind someone else reading; secrecy will always look bad.

A deputy head teacher at a primary school

> My preparation involved looking further than my job description and preparing what I wanted to say. For example, I wanted to be involved in policy making and looked to see if the job description covered this. You have to be *au fait* with the organisation. Know your subject when you're questioned and try and anticipate any questions thoroughly. For instance, they may want to know how you would deal with a trade union problem. Anyone moving into management must be able to communicate ideas and have good interpersonal skills. So it's important to appear positive without seeming overforceful.

Preparing for the interview

The interview is not a normal social interaction, and thus it requires an approach reserved for this specific type of situation. The aim of the interviewer(s) is to assess how far your personality, skills and experience fit the job requirements. You have to convince them that you are the best person for the job. The interview is also a chance for you to find out everything you can about the job, possibly meet the people you will be working with, and find out about career prospects.

You do not want to be left speechless by an unexpected question. Nor do you want to give the impression that you are not really interested by failing to ask any questions of your own. It pays to be prepared.

There are four stages in preparing for the interview. They are the following:

1. Research the organisation.

2. Prepare your answers.

3. Prepare your questions.

4. Prepare for the 'first 30 seconds'.

Research the organisation

The most important preparation for an interview is to find out about the organisation that you hope to work for. You can do this in the following ways:

- Telephone the organisation's public relations department

and ask for basic promotional literature and the annual report, if applicable. The department will usually be very willing to oblige.

- Find out from business directories how the business operates and whether it is expanding, its main competitors, and any special characteristics which you find particularly interesting. Most public libraries have a selection of business directories.
- If you do find some interesting facts and figures to quote at the interview, make sure they are up-to-date!
- Read the national and local papers for any current developments about the organisation, or the market it operates in.

Try to find out the following information:

- what the organisation produces or sells;
- whether it is successful;
- its main competitors;
- number of employees;
- location of headquarters/regional branches;
- future plans.

A little homework will stand you in good stead; and, apart from anything else, it is complimentary to your future employers if you can show an informed interest in, and understanding of, their activities.

Prepare your answers

Obviously, you cannot anticipate all the questions that you might be asked, but there is no doubt that some questions are asked more frequently than others, and you can prepare answers to these. Here are the ten questions which are most commonly asked at interviews.

Top ten interview questions

1.   Tell me about yourself.

2.   Why do you want this job?

3.   What would you say have been your main achievements in your present job?

4. Why are you leaving your present job?

5. What do you regard as your particular strengths?

6. What are your weaknesses?

7. What sort of career challenge are you looking for now?

8. What do you see yourself doing in five years' time?

9. What can you offer this organisation?

10. How would you change things if you were appointed?

Let us see what kind of information you are expected to supply in answer to these questions.

1. *Tell me about yourself*

Be relevant and concise. Do not waffle. Summarise the following points:

- profession/occupation;
- main areas of experience/expertise;
- main qualities and skills.

If you are not sure how much detail the interviewer requires, you could say something such as the following: 'I'm quite happy to expand on any of these areas, if you wish me to' or 'How far back would you like me to go?' Do not be afraid to ask for more information to enable you to answer a question adequately. The interviewer may not necessarily be as well prepared as you are!

2. *Why do you want this job?*

Surprisingly, this is a question that candidates often overlook when preparing what they are going to say. Ask yourself why this particular job appeals to you. What makes you so suitable for the post? What combination of experience, skills, interests and knowledge makes you ideal for the job? Try to show how your desire for this particular post coincides with what the organisation is looking for. For example, if you know that the organisation is looking for somebody to bring a creative and innovative approach to the job, then stress the fact that you have lots of new ideas that you would like to incorporate into your work. Give an example of how you were able to do this in your present or former job.

3. *What would you say have been your main achievements in your present job?*

Try to identify two or three ways in which you are able to demonstrate that you have leadership qualities. This is particularly important if you are applying for your first management post. Go back to the skills check-list you completed in Chapter 1, and look at your strongest area. Summarise the ways in which you have been able to use these skills at work. It may have been by leading a successful team, solving a particularly tricky problem, introducing a new way of working, implementing change successfully, or seeing through a project from start to finish. Whatever it is, do not underrate your achievements. An interview is not the place for false modesty.

4. *Why are you leaving your present job?*

Try to give positive rather than negative reasons for leaving your present organisation, reasons such as wanting a change of direction, more responsibility, or an opportunity to use and develop your skills. Never run down a previous employer or organisation. The interviewers will assume that you are likely to do this again.

5. *What do you regard as your particular strengths?*

This is your big opportunity to show how your skills, qualities and experiences make you a perfect match for the job. Be positive, but avoid boasting. Using all the information that you have about your own abilities, outline the management skills that you have that make you particularly suitable for the job.

6. *What are your weaknesses?*

What you should not do at this point is to sigh with relief at the opportunity to say what you cannot do, and then provide the interviewers with a catalogue of disasters. If you are aware that you do not meet all the job requirements, say so. Then go on to explain how you think you can overcome these problems by further training, experience, etc. Doing this will not necessarily rule you out of the job. You would not have been given an interview if it was felt that you were not suitable. Therefore make the most of this opportunity to show how you can excel — if given a chance.

7. *What sort of career challenge are you looking for now?*

Go back to the job description and try to match your 'career challenge' with the requirements and development of the job. At this point you have an opportunity to ask about future prospects. Show that you are undaunted by the prospect of 'challenge', seeing it as an opportunity to show what you can bring to the job.

8. *What do you see yourself doing in five years' time?*

The important thing here is to show that you have given the question some thought. If you have an ultimate goal in mind, explain what you hope to do. If not, try to describe what you are looking for in a career. Do not give the impression that you do not have a clue. If you do not know what you want to do in five years' time, try to demonstrate an attitude which is flexible enough to take advantage of new opportunities.

9. *What can you offer this organisation?*

For this question, as with a number of others, the exercises you completed in Chapter 1 are all-important. Look at your skills, qualities and experience, and consider to what extent they match the job description. Modify them if necessary to place emphasis on the skills you have that the organisation is looking for. This is your opportunity to demonstrate how well qualified you are for this particular post. Make the most of it!

10. *How would you change things if you were appointed?*

A tricky question. Be careful. You need to ask yourself what the organisation is really looking for. A newcomer who seeks to change things may be an asset or a threat. If the organisation is undergoing some sort of change, it may specifically be looking for new people in order to introduce a new approach. Ask yourself what the problems seem to be, and how you think a new approach could help. Be cautious about suggesting sweeping changes, particularly as you might not have adequate background knowledge. Discuss your approach, by all means, but do not assure the MD that you can solve all the problems of the organisation!

These are just some of the questions that you may be asked. If you have taken the time to consider them beforehand, you will not be at a loss when they are asked. Aim to give thoughtful answers to all the questions — without rambling and talking yourself out of the job. And do not be afraid of silences. They can lead to regrets if you fill them with ill-considered statements. Throughout all these questions, bear in mind the following question:

'What can I offer this organisation?'

Identify what the interviewers want — and show them how well you fill the bill.

Now, here is the third type of preparation that you can do — prepare some questions of your own.

Prepare your questions

Remember that the interview selection process is mutual. You want to feel confident that you can do the job properly and fit into the organisation as much as the interviewers do. Therefore make the most of the opportunity to ask questions. The question, 'Is there anything that you would like to ask us?', generally comes at the end of the interview. Try to use the time to show that you are interested and to clarify anything that you are unsure about. Phrase your questions carefully. Here are some suggestions:

Ten questions to ask at the interview

1. How did the vacancy arise?

2. Whom will I be responsible for/to?

3. What sorts of problems might I meet on the job?

4. Does the organisation have a policy on —— ?

5. What is the accepted style of management?

6. Are there any facilities for —— ?

7. What opportunities exist for further training?

8. What prospects are there for further promotion?

9. How and when will I learn the results of my application?

10. What is the salary attached to this post?

Do not be afraid to ask about money. It may not be your main reason for wanting the job, but it is still an important factor.

These are general questions that you may be able to use. However, it is more than likely that you will have your own questions which are linked to the specific job and organisation you are applying to.

Finally, prepare for the first 30 seconds of the interview.

Prepare for the first 30 seconds

Management consultants say that most decisions to hire are made in the first 30 seconds of the interview. This is a daunting prospect, and it means that the immediate impression that you make must be the right one. In order to get off to a good start, you have to look good and establish good rapport with your interviewers.

How to survive the first 30 seconds

1. Reread the job advertisement, your CV, and any questions and answers you have written in preparation. They will all make you feel confident.

2. Shake hands firmly. Practice shaking hands beforehand.

3. Make eye contact with your interviewer(s).

4. Smile in a friendly manner — not a broad grin, just a pleasant gesture.

5. Sit down when you are asked to.

You are now ready to begin the interview.

The interview itself

Here are some ideas on how to conduct yourself at the

interview. They are tried and tested ideas taken from women who have been through the process and found that they worked.

Dos and don'ts for interviews

DO make sure your image fits the company, without changing your appearance, style and manner totally.

DO wear a 'quiet' outfit with a touch of brightness — a blouse or scarf, for example.

DO ensure you have researched the company thoroughly — if there are any facts you are not sure about, do not use them.

DO take a book or magazine to read while you are waiting — something small enough to slip into your bag when your name is called.

DO remember that the interview process starts as soon as you walk into the building — power resides in unlikely places.

DO be friendly and pleasant at all times with everyone you meet in the organisation.

DO be alert and interested — if you are faced with an interview panel, look at the speaker when a question is being asked.

DO be positive, without appearing over-confident — providing too much detail about yourself and your achievements can be just as damaging as providing too little.

DO talk about your interests, particularly if they can be related to the tasks you hope to be doing in your new job.

DO about 70 per cent of the talking. Experts vary on the amount they recommend, but 70 per cent is a good guideline. If you are interviewed on a one-to-one basis, this percentage may increase.

DON'T forget to go to the lavatory before the interview starts!

DON'T arrive too late — or too early. If your journey is delayed for any reason, phone to apologise and explain. If you are going to be early, find somewhere locally to have a coffee.

DON'T force humour by making jokes — but show your appreciation of any 'witty' comments made by the interviewer.

DON'T smoke — even if you are offered a cigarette.

DON'T fidget or wriggle. Sit in an upright but relaxed way. If you have an annoying habit such as fiddling with rings or touching your hair when nervous, be aware of these and make a conscious effort to keep your hands still.

DON'T fold your arms — it looks defensive.

DON'T bluff your way through a question you did not understand — ask for clarification. And *never* lie.

DON'T be modest about your achievements — if you did a good job, say so. If you have evidence of tangible results, so much the better.

DON'T lose your temper if asked a provocative question.

DON'T forget to thank the interviewer(s) and say goodbye — the final 30 seconds are nearly as important as the first.

The advice you have just read has been given by women with experience in the recruitment and selection process. Remember that interviews are not necessarily fair, and can be subject to the bias and preconceptions of the interviewer. Be aware, also, that the interviewer may not be skilled at doing the job, may be less well prepared than you are — and just as nervous!

Be yourself. Do what you think is right for you, and you will not let yourself down. If you look upon the interview as a learning experience, you will gain something from it — even if you do not get the job. On the subject of questions — give thoughtful answers to the questions asked. If you object to any of them, say so, directly but politely.

Coping with difficult questions

Do not be thrown off balance by unexpected questions or comments. And, certainly, do not lose your temper — even when provoked. You may be tempted to lose your cool, particularly if you are asked questions such as the following:

- What about child-minding arrangements?
- Are you hoping to have family?
- Can a woman cope with the demands of this job?
- I see that you haven't been employed as a manager before?
- What does your husband think about —— ?

The questions may be simply offensive, or they may be asked deliberately to test your reaction. Either way, answer politely, truthfully and assertively. Employers should not ask these questions, but they sometimes do. Therefore be prepared with your answers. If you think that the odds are stacked against you, try to tackle their reservations in a non-defensive manner. Here are three examples of what you could say.

Example 1

If you think the interviewers are implying that a woman may not be able to do the job, you could say something such as the following:

I am quite used to working with men, and have always had good working relationships with them. I haven't found that either my credibility or my ability to do the job has been affected by the fact that I am a woman. Once people realise that I am efficient and good at my job, they accept me for what I am.'

Example 2

If it is mentioned that you have not been employed in management before, you could say:

Yes that's true. But, as you can see from my previous experience, I have supervised staff in my capacity as volunteer organiser for a local fund-raising group, and we were able to exceed the targets which had been set.

Or you could refer to any type of activity, at home or at work, in or out of paid employment, when you were able to use managerial skills.

Example 3

If you are asked about child-minding arrangements or your plans for a family, try responding in one of the following ways:

Could you tell me how this is relevant to the job I've applied for?

or

Do you put this question to your male candidates?

You could also ask the interviewers to repeat the question, thus giving them an opportunity to rethink what they have said.

Whatever you say, bear in mind that it is in your own interest to be polite and assertive when you respond to the questions asked. You may decide that you would rather not answer if you object to a particular question. If that is the case, say so. Your decision should be based on your personal feelings and how much you want this particular job.

Remember — no matter how well suited you are to the job, if you fail to present yourself well at the interview you will not get the job. You do not get a second chance to make a good first impression.

Finally, let us look at how to cope if you do not get the post for which you have been interviewed.

Coping with disappointment

Before looking at ways of coping with disappointment, remember that there is a large element of luck in the outcome of interviews. Just because you did not get the job, you should not think that you are worthless as a person. Do not mope or tell yourself that you are not any good. There is no surer way to destroy your self-confidence.

Listed below are four steps which will help you move forward positively.

Coping with disappointment — step by step

Release your feelings It is unrealistic to say, do not be disappointed or do not feel frustrated or angry. It is inevitable that you will have feelings of this kind, particularly if you feel that you were treated badly or unfairly, or if you were misled about the nature of the job. You may also feel annoyed with yourself for having made 'foolish' mistakes. Work through these feelings alone, or with someone you can talk to, and then move on to the next step.

Evaluate your performance You can learn a lot about yourself by analysing what might have gone wrong, and what went right. You should not assume, unless you know for sure, that anything did, in fact, go wrong. You may not have been chosen for lots of reasons, some of which may not have been within your control. If the letter of rejection does not indicate why you were not selected, try making contact with one of the interviewers in order to discover how your technique may be improved. They may be willing to pass on some tips which could help you next time round.

If you think you can improve your own interview performance, it makes sense to go back over it. There is a check-list for doing this at the end of this chapter.

Talk constructively to yourself The way you think about yourself may well affect your ability to get the next job, particularly if you allow negative thinking to undermine your confidence. For example, suppose your reaction after a rejection was this: 'I should have walked into that job, and now here I am, back where I started. I'm not suited for a management job . . . I can't suffer this humiliation again.' In this response you would be talking yourself out of what could be a very successful career — next time around.

It is never very easy to cope with 'failure', particularly when you feel you have to convince people that you know you can do better next time. But you do not do yourself any good by labelling yourself a 'failure' because you fail to get the job you want first — or even 21st — time around. Managers have to learn to take all sorts of failures and rejections in their stride, and thus it is important not to lose confidence in yourself when this happens.

A more positive reaction is expressed by the following: 'I am disappointed. It would have been good to have got the job, particularly as I'd prepared so well. However, because I have been rejected this time round, doesn't make me a failure. I'll see what I can learn from my mistakes in order not to make them again.'

Find a way forward In order to improve your interview technique, you might like to try the following suggestions:

- practise answering/asking questions with a friend;
- practise by answering/asking these questions, using a tape recorder;
- complete the interview evaluation check-list at the end of this chapter. It will also be useful for you to refer to before each interview.

Once you have answered these questions, you will have identified the areas where you are satisfactory, and those where you need to improve for your next interview. Based on this information, you can then draw up an action plan which will provide you with specific things to do in preparation for your next interview.

Finally, do not give up!

No interview is a waste of time. By going for a few interviews you will get an insight into how different organisations operate, and what they expect of their managers. Active interviewing means that you should recognise the right job for you when it comes along. When you go for the interview, nine times out of ten, you have as much chance as anyone else of getting the job — otherwise you would not be there. And with all your experience of interviews, you will not have to go to as much trouble to convince the interviewers that you are the one for their job.

Interview evaluation check-list

After each interview, when you have relieved your feelings and regained your sense of perspective, read through these questions. Make a tick for 'yes' and a cross for 'no'.

Was I confident? ☐

Did I look my best? ☐

☐ Was I relaxed?

☐ Did I smile?

☐ Did I make eye contact?

☐ Did I speak directly and without undue hesitation?

☐ Was I enthusiastic?

☐ Did I answer questions clearly and concisely?

☐ Did I give full answers?

☐ Did I give examples of initiatives I'd taken?

☐ Did I take advantage of 'cues' I was given to show what I could do?

☐ Did I remain calm?

☐ Did I emphasise my strengths?

☐ Did I relate my skills to the job I was being interviewed for?

☐ Did I give examples of my experience?

☐ Did I offer extra information?

☐ Did I ask questions?

☐ Did I handle difficult questions well?

☐ Did I convince them that I really wanted the job?

☐ Did I convince them that I could really do the job?

☐ Was I as well prepared as I should have been?

5

Settling In

The first day, the first week, and even the first month can be
a traumatic time for anyone embarking on a new career. They
can also be the most exciting and challenging. You are not only
a new starter; you are also a new manager. And because of this
all eyes are turned your way — you are in the limelight.

Think back to before you became a manager. How did you
feel when you got a new 'boss'? Were you wary, a little
nervous, and concerned that the new manager would over-
turn all the good practices which were in place? You can be
sure that your new subordinates are experiencing the same
feelings that you did then.

To compound matters, you are a woman, and, even today,
certain staff will find it difficult to accept a female manager.
Some people may even be downright uncooperative.

This chapter looks at the problems you may encounter as
you start your new job — and suggests some strategies for
coping, for getting through that first day, week and month.

FIRST IMPRESSIONS

When you start a new management job, it is important to
establish yourself as a competent and confident leader as
quickly as possible. What you do in the first few weeks will
shape the way in which people respond to you in the future.

When a woman moves into a managerial position, some
people will regard her less as an individual and more as a

stereotype of whom they have preconceived ideas. Many may expect a woman to be weaker; some may be hostile to an assertive woman; others may sneer at the idea of working for a woman. If, coupled with the 'disadvantages' of being female, the new manager also happens to be young, well qualified, new to the company, attractive, and the first woman to hold the post or to take up a newly created position, the people she will be working with may have further reason to resent her.

If the idea of 'being in charge' also seems alien to a woman's own self-image, she is going to have problems in developing a leadership style with which she feels comfortable.

Strategies

Do not be discouraged. There are ways in which you can overcome some of the problems you may encounter in your new job. Here are six ways in which you can establish your authority and get off to the best possible start in your new role.

Six ways to start well

1.   Accept your authority.

2.   Ask for information.

3.   Project a confident image and style.

4.   Communicate openly and directly.

5.   Get to know your staff as individuals.

6.   Do not make quick judgements or changes.

Accept your authority

When you are newly promoted, it may seem strange at first to think of yourself in this higher position. You may have doubts about your ability to do the job, and hesitate to take hold of the reins. The way to counteract this type of self-doubt is to think positively. Here are four examples.

Example 1

Negative thinking:

I don't know whether I'm the right person for the job.

Positive thinking:

I was selected for this post because senior managers thought I was the best person for the job. I have experience and qualities which I can draw upon.

Example 2

Negative thinking:

I don't like bossing people around.

Positive thinking:

Being in charge doesn't mean that I have to adopt an aggressive role. The job carries with it certain responsibilities which I have the authority to carry out. I may not be used to this type of role, but I can learn and improve with practice.

Example 3

Negative thinking:

I might get it wrong.

Positive thinking:

I'm bound to make some mistakes, but I can learn from them. I don't know anybody who doesn't make a mistake at some time, so why should I be any different?

Example 4

Negative thinking:

If I get it all wrong they'll say it's because I'm a woman.

Positive thinking:

A woman is as well qualified as any man to do this job. I've got some of the qualities of my male colleagues — and some that they lack. I've got lots of ideas for making the job a success. Someone has to do the job. Why not I?

Try to apply this positive way of thinking if you find yourself assailed by doubts in your new role. You will find that it works!

Ask for information

If you are promoted into an area, department or organisation with which you are unfamiliar, you will be starting off as a 'learner'. There will be specific things that you do not know and many things that will take some months to find out. You may be tempted to pretend that you know more than you do, in order not to be dependent on other people for help or information.

On the other hand, you can use your newness to your own advantage. Find out as much as you can by talking to people within your department. Ask questions — lots of questions. Make use of their knowledge and experience and let them know their help is appreciated.

Another way of settling in more easily is to find out more about the culture of the organisation. What are the norms? These are unwritten rules about what people should or should not do. To identify these, you need to observe colleagues and other staff. How do managers dress? Where do they have lunch? Do they hold formal or informal meetings? Do staff take breaks? What is the attitude towards lateness? Do people take work home? What hours do people work? Norms are often difficult to follow in the early days of a new job. Probably the best tactic is to observe colleagues and other staff until you have made up your mind which types of behaviour you are willing to copy or encourage, and which ones you may wish to change.

Project a confident image and style

If you want to be seen as competent, you have to project a confident self-image. If you think of yourself as inferior, incapable or inadequate, you will appear so to other people. The way you sit, talk, dress and stand all say something about the type of person that you are. Be sure that the image that you are projecting to other people is one with which you feel comfortable.

Having confidence in your style also applies to your style of management. Problems can arise if your predecessor had a style which was very different from the one you prefer. Your staff may expect you to adopt a similar style of managing — and be confused when you do not. Explain how your style differs and why. This way, when their expectations are not met, they may be pleasantly surprised.

Communicate openly and directly

One of the best ways of avoiding hostility and resentment, particularly when you are new to the job, is to encourage an atmosphere of open and direct communication. If you sense any ill-feeling towards you, confront it. If you do not, it will continue and may undermine your leadership role. If you feel that a person is having difficulty in accepting you as manager, it is far better to confront the situation than to ignore it and hope the problem will go away. The chances are it will not — it will only get worse. By confronting the situation, you give other people the opportunity to voice any fears or anxieties that they may have about your role.

If you encourage your staff to articulate their worries, the chances are that you will be aware of any problems. One of the unhealthiest atmospheres for anybody to work in is one in which there is no trust between manager and staff. This type of communication failure ultimately affects everybody's performance at work. Your openness and willingness to listen will remove much suspicion, misconception and distrust.

Get to know your staff as individuals

Remember that although you are responsible for a 'team', this team is made of individuals, and you need to see them as such. On your first day, be sure to introduce yourself to each member of the team. This small gesture acknowledges the fact that you value them, irrespective of their status. Take some time during the first few weeks in the job to meet and talk directly with each member of your staff in order to find out:

- their responsibilities;
- their work problems;
- their areas of expertise;
- their job expectations;
- their suggested improvements to the job.

This will enable you to build up a picture of each individual, as well as helping you to plan your strategies for future ways of working. Be aware, though, that speaking to individuals in this way is only the first step. You will have created expectations in them which they will expect you to follow up. There is a responsibility on both sides to work towards departmental objectives in the most effective way. If there are problems in the department, you and the team will have to apply some creative thinking to solve them. By asking about career aspirations, you have made the first move in helping to develop your staff. You will receive much information as a result of this type of interview which should help you to decide on future action. Give yourself some time to consider what should be done.

Do not make quick judgements or changes

Wait for a while before you take action. The proverb that a new broom sweeps clean is not always appropriate. New managers are always keen to implement new ideas and to make their mark, but such innovation can be a mistake if the changes are not prepared for or, indeed, needed. Take time to observe and to think about what you see before you decide to make any changes. If some of the norms, such as long tea breaks, using the telephone for personal calls during working hours, or a too tolerant attitude towards lateness, seem unreasonable to you, wait a while before deciding what action to take. You may instigate changes which remedy the problem but which cost dearly in terms of productivity and damaged relationships. If you make it clear that you are going to wait before making changes, people will appreciate your consideration, and this will add to your credibility as a manager.

If you have given some thought to the strategies you will adopt during your first days and weeks in your new role, you are more likely to ease into your role and to establish your authority and credibility as an effective manager. Here is some advice from other women managers on how they settled in to their management role:

Case studies

Catherine Taylor, Learning Consultant, Shell UK

When you are settling in, it's important to go on a data-gathering exercise to help you carry out the job efficiently. I think getting to know the people and how the operation works is essential. If you're managing a team, sit down with your staff and discuss the running of the department. It's important to believe that the people working for you will do the best job they can and that you give them the opportunity to prove it.

Kate Maddock, Personnel Officer, Training, Massey Ferguson, Coventry

Try to remember as many names as possible and take in as much detail as you can, so you appear professional and friendly. People watch you on your first day to see what you are like — so act the part. First impressions count, so if you build up a rapport and take time out to talk to people, even if it's not work related, they get the feeling that they can approach you.

Action Plan

Now it is time to draw up your personal action plan — things you are going to start doing — or stop doing — in your own preparations to enter management. To help you formulate your plan, you may like to refer to the exercises you have completed throughout this book. You may like to look at:

- the skills check-list;
- the statements you made on accepting yourself;
- the guidelines for liking yourself;
- the step-by-step approach to making the most of yourself;
- your work values;
- your career goal;
- your CV;
- the interview evaluation check-list.

Here is an extract from one woman's action plan:

Things I am going to start/stop doing	Made a start	Getting there	Doing well
1. Stop saying sorry all the time	✓ 5 Sept		
2. Sort through clothes; throw out what I don't wear	✓ 7 Sept	✓ 20 Sept	
3. Write my CV	✓ 9 Sept	10 Sept	*done!*

To write your own action plan, follow the steps outlined below.

Writing an action plan — step by step

1. Select *three* things you are going to start or stop doing in your personal preparations for management. You might like to start with something relatively easy, to boost your confidence.

2. Write them down the left-hand column.

3. Come back to the list in a week and review progress.

4. When you have achieved what you resolved to do, tick the column and date it.

5. When you have achieved your goal on three occasions or have completed the task you set yourself, you are entitled to feel pleased with your progress. You have achieved what you set out to do.

6. As you complete one task, add others to the bottom of the list — an action plan is an ongoing process.

The secret is not to work on too many tasks at one time. Take things one step at a time and progress to more difficult areas later rather than sooner.

Some blank action plan sheets follow for you to use.

Action plan

Things I am going to start/stop doing	Made a start	Getting there	Doing well

Action plan

Things I am going to start/stop doing	Made a start	Getting there	Doing well

If you find the changes you make are effective, they will probably become part of your normal pattern of behaviour within a short time.

If you find that something does not work immediately, do not give up too soon. Persevere, as certain changes take time — particularly those concerned with developing a new, confident you!

If certain things do not seem to work, look for other techniques that work for you. An action plan is an ongoing process, so come back to it from time to time and make the changes which suit you.

Good luck in preparing for your management career!

You may like to read the next two books in the series:

The Successful Manager
Getting to the Top.

Further Reading

Alkenson, Jacqueline (1988) *Coping with Stress at Work*, Thorsons, Wellingborough.

Armstrong, Michael (1990) *How to be an Even Better Manager*, Kogan Page, London.

Bryce, Lee (1989) *The Influential Woman*, Piatkus, London.

Chambers, C, Cooper, S and McLean, A (1990) *Develop Your Management Potential*, Kogan Page, London.

Chapman, Elwood (1988) *How to Develop a Positive Attitude*, Kogan Page, London.

Cooper, Cary and Davidson, Marilyn (1984) *Women in Management*, Heinemann, London.

—— and Lewis, S (1989) *Career Couples*, Unwin, London.

Courtis, John (1988) *44 Most Common Management Mistakes*, Kogan Page, London.

Crabtree, Stan (1991) *Moving Up*, Kogan Page, London.

Davidson, Marylin (1985) *Reach for the Top*, Piatkus, London.

Dickson, Ann (1985) *A Woman in Your Own Right*, Quartet, London.

Dyer, Wayne (1985) *Pulling Your Own Strings*, Hamlyn, Twickenham.

—— (1986) *Your Erroneous Zone*, Sphere, London.

Ernst & Young (1991) *The Manager's Self-Assessment Kit*, Kogan Page, London.

Evans, R and Russell, P (1989) *The Creative Manager*, Unwin, London.

Fisher, Roger and Ury, William (1986) *Getting to Yes*, Hutchinson, London.

Haddock, Patricia and Manning, Marylyn (1989) *Leadership Skills for Women*, Kogan Page, London.

Hansard Society Commission (1990) *Women at the Top*, Hansard Society, London.

Haynes, Marion (1988) *Effective Meeting Skills*, Kogan Page, London.

Lindley, Patricia and Makin, Peter (1991) *Positive Stress Management*, Kogan Page, London.

Lloyd, Sam (1988) *How to Develop Assertiveness*, Kogan Page, London.

McDonald, Janet (1986) *Climbing the Ladder*, Methuen, London.

Minzberg, Henry (1973) *The Nature of Managerial Work*, Harper and Row, New York.

Moates-Kennedy, Marilyn (1984) *Powerbase: How to Build It, How to Keep It*, Fawcett Crest, Wetherby.

Morris, M J (1988) *First Time Manager*, Kogan Page, London.

National Economic Development Office (NEDO) (1990) *Women Managers*, Kogan Page, London.

Paul, Nancy (1984) *The Right to be You*, Chartwell Bratt, Bromley.

Powell, G N (1988) *Women and Men in Management*, Sage, London.

Rhodes, J and Thame, S (1988) *The Colours of Your Mind*, Fontana, London.

Shaevitz, Marjorie (1984) *The Superwoman Syndrome*, Fontana, London.

Siewart, Lothar (1989) *Managing Your Time*, Kogan Page, London.

Skinner, Jane and Fritchie, Rennie (1988) *Working Choices*, J M Dent, London.

Spenser, L and Young, K (1990) *Women Managers in Local Government: Removing the Barriers*, LGMB, London.

Women Returners' Network (1991) *Returning to Work*, Kogan Page, London.

Further Information

Business in the Community
227A City Road
London EC1
Tel: 071-253 3716

Confederation of British
  Industry
Centre Point
103 New Oxford Street
London WC1A 1DU
Tel: 071-379 7400

Domino Consultancy Ltd
56 Charnwood Road
Shepshed
Leicestershire LE12 9NP
Tel: 0509 505404

Equal Opportunities
  Commission
Overseas House
Quay Street
Manchester M3 3HN
Tel: 061-833 9244

European Women's
  Management Development
  Network
EWMD Secretariat
c/o EFMD
40 Rue Washington
B-1050 Brussels
Belgium
UK Secretary: Christine
  Barham
Tel: 0442 843491

Industrial Society: Pepperell
  Unit
Robert Hyde House
48 Bryanston Square
London W1H 7LN
Tel: 071-262 2401

Trade Union Congress
Great Russell Street
London WC1
Tel: 071-636 4030

United Kingdom Federation of
  Business and Professional
  Women
23 Ansdell Street
London W8 5BN
Tel: 071-938 1729

Women in Management
64 Marryat Road
Wimbledon
London SW19 5BN
Tel: 081-944 6332